Business English/30

Colleen B. Kish
Education Specialist
Special Services Division
State Department of Education
St. Paul, Minnesota

Gregg Division/McGraw-Hill Book Company

New York Atlanta Dallas St. Louis San Francisco
Auckland Bogotá Düsseldorf London
Madrid Mexico Montreal New Delhi Panama
Paris São Paulo Singapore Sydney Tokyo Toronto

Senior Editor / Joseph Tinervia
Editing Supervisor / Michael J. Esposito
Production Supervisor / Frank Bellantoni
Design Supervisor / Caryl Valerie Spinka

Interior Designer / Gregory Clark
Cover Designer / Jorge Hernandez
Illustrator / Barbara Maslen

Library of Congress Cataloging in Publication Data

Kish, Colleen B
Business English/30.

Includes index.
1. English language—Business English. 2. English language—Grammar—date. I. Title.
PE1115.K57 808'.066651021 79-27742
ISBN 0-07-034842-1

BUSINESS ENGLISH/30

12 13 14 15 DODO 8 9 8 7

To the Student

When business executives are asked which skills and abilities they value most in their employees, they always place communication skills high on the list. Why do employers put priority on the ability to write and speak correctly and on other language skills? The reason is simple: Employers know that business workers spend most of their on-the-job time communicating—communicating with other employees, with clients and customers, and with suppliers. As you can see, then, communication skills will greatly affect your ability to get, keep, and advance on a job.

Business English/30 is designed to give you a head start in your business career by helping you to review basic principles of English *as they apply to today's business office*. In other words, *Business English/30* does not emphasize the theory or the history of the English language, nor does it give a detailed, technical presentation of linguistics. Instead, *Business English/30* concentrates on the correct use of English in everyday, routine situations. It stresses the principles that you *must* know to write and speak correctly.

Specifically, *Business English/30* is designed to help you reach these overall goals:

1. To avoid the most common communication errors.
2. To understand and use correct sentence structure.
3. To punctuate sentences correctly and to use capitalization properly.
4. To improve your spelling of some commonly used business words.

As you will see, more-specific goals are listed at the beginning of each text section, so that you will always know the objectives of the lessons within that section. Use these as your personal goals in this course. By achieving the goals section by section, you will prepare yourself to handle all your on-the-job communication duties confidently and effectively. In addition, two or three tests will allow you to document your own progress. Your teacher may give you a Survey Quiz at the beginning of this course and a Final Exam at the end. Together, these two tests, with the Midterm Exam, will show you how much progress you have made in achieving your goals.

As you study each lesson in *Business English/30*, be sure to take advantage of the reference tools that every business writer uses—a dictionary and a style manual. Develop the habit of using them whenever you must check spelling, capitalization, letter style, usage, and so on. The authorities used for *Business English/30* are *Webster's New Collegiate Dictionary* (G. & C. Merriam Co., Springfield, Massachusetts, 1979) and *The Gregg Reference Manual*, Fifth Edition, by William A. Sabin (Gregg Division, McGraw-Hill Book Company, New York, 1977).

Colleen B. Kish

Contents

Units of Communication

YOUR GOALS

After finishing this section, you will be able to:

1. Identify the seven basic units of communication.
2. Identify the subject and the action/condition parts of a sentence.
3. Write declarative, questioning, and exclamatory sentences.
4. Recognize and correct unfinished or split sentences.
5. Correctly spell and use 15 frequently misspelled words.

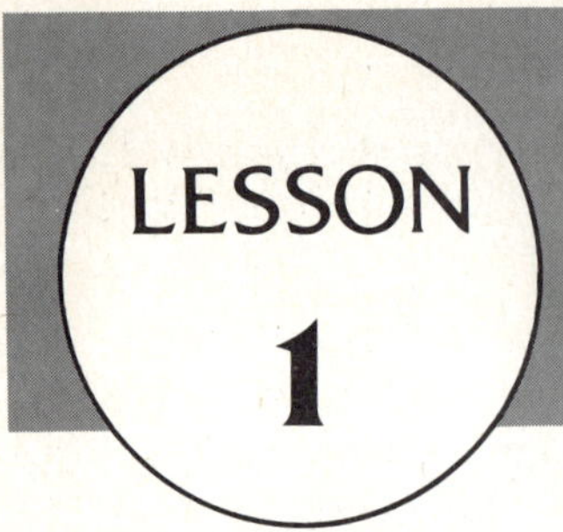

Words and Their Uses

Can you read the following famous quotation?

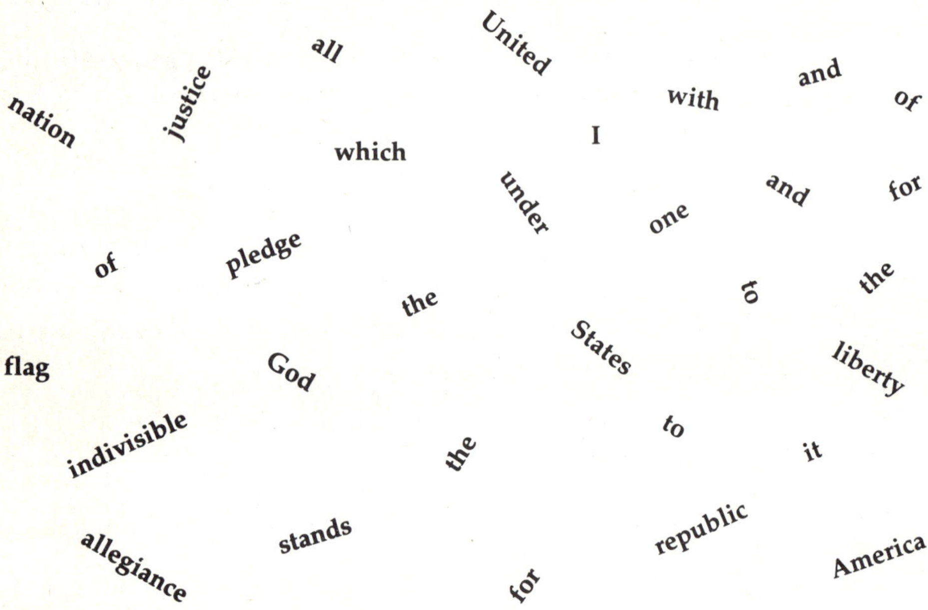

Confusing, isn't it? How about the same words in this pattern?

with	indivisible	republic	the	flag	the
liberty	God	for	to	of	to
and	under	which	and	the	allegiance
justice	nation	it	America	United	pledge
for	one	stands	of	States	I
all					

Still not clear? (It is if you read up and down and backwards.) Then how about reading the words in this arrangement?

ipledgeallegiancetotheflagoftheunitedstatesofamericaandtotherepublicfor whichitstandsonenationunderGodindivisiblewithlibertyandjusticeforall

Are you still having trouble reading the quotation? Maybe this pattern will be easier to understand.

I pledge allegiance to the flag of the United States of America and to the republic for which it stands; one nation under God, indivisible, with liberty and justice for all.

You can see that the letters and words are the same in all the examples, yet they are hard to read when they aren't put together in a familiar way. When you read the quotation, you can't pay attention to the message because you're too busy thinking about the pattern or the order of the words themselves.

When you write or speak, you need to remember this fact. To get your ideas across—to impress a possible employer, to make a sale, to influence an audience, to get a "yes" answer—you must be in control of your messages.

The following review of word usage and sentence structure—think of them as *patterns*—will help you build your *word power.* And word power can make you a success!

Let's start with words, the basic unit of communication. They generally can be grouped into seven categories according to the way you use them in delivering a message.

NOUNS

Nouns identify persons, places, things, or ideas. Many nouns have body and shape; they can be seen or felt. They can do things or have things done to them.

employee horse book street football rain Susan Miami

Other nouns are ideas—things we identify in our minds.

fun time power liberty freedom health love

Here is an example of how nouns can be used in a message:

I felt *fear* when the *elevator* stopped between *floors.*

Checkup 1. Underline each noun.

1. Karen has a calculator on her desk.
2. The story was about politics and power.
3. My sister got a job in Nebraska.

PRONOUNS

Pronouns take the place of nouns. They provide a shortcut you can use to avoid repeating nouns. Here are some pronouns you use every day:

I you he she it we they
me him her us them

my/mine your/yours his hers its
our/ours their/theirs

As you speak, you automatically substitute pronouns for nouns. For example:

Bob Conrad and ~~Bob Conrad's~~ his brother went to ~~Bob Conrad and Bob Conrad's brother's~~ their mother's house to see if ~~Bob Conrad and Bob Conrad's brother's mother~~ she needed any help.

Checkup 2. Underline each pronoun.

1. I told her that we should go to their party.
2. Although the grass is long, you need not mow it yet.
3. Kerry said he would give her the letters from his desk.

VERBS

Verbs can show either action or condition (the "being") of a noun or a pronoun.

Action Verbs. Most verbs are action verbs: *run, give, speak, hurried, spoke, typed,* and *won.*

We *run* several miles before breakfast each day.
Mr. Trent and Ms. Klein always *give* generously to the United Fund.
For more information, *speak* to your supervisor.
Annette *hurried* to the train station.

Checkup 3. Underline each action verb.

1. When I ride the bus, I arrive early.
2. Kent jumped into the car and drove away.
3. They hired an accountant and filed a complaint.

Being Verbs. A few verbs don't show any action at all. Rather, they show that something exists. They are called *being verbs.*

He *is* our friend. Jan *was* friendly. I *am* lost.
Those clouds *are* threatening. They *were* sorry.

Here is a complete list of the being verbs: *am, is, are, was, were, be, been,* and *being.*

Checkup 4. Underline each being verb.

1. The work was easy, but the salary was too low.
2. I am unhappy here, just as they were.
3. You are my first choice; she is my second choice.

Condition Verbs. A few special verbs tell something about the condition of a noun. Several of these involve our senses, for example, the verbs *feel, look, hear, taste,* and *smell.*

The peaches *taste* sour. She *looks* tired.
The day *seems* long. I *felt* restless.

Checkup 5. Underline each condition verb.

1. The house looks old.
2. The room felt cold, but the hall seemed warm.
3. I felt confident, but my story sounded ridiculous.

Verb Phrases. Sometimes verbs work in pairs or in groups to show an action or a condition. These combinations are called *verb phrases.*

Water *was running* down the wall.
We *had been working* very hard.
They *will have been traveling* for eight months.

Checkup 6. Underline each verb phrase.

1. The group will leave for Toledo today.
2. Arlis will be driving, but Sharon will be flying.
3. They have been trying to consolidate for years.

ADJECTIVES

Adjectives describe or point to a noun. They give additional information that helps the reader to get an accurate or a clear understanding of the noun.

Leading Adjectives. Most adjectives "lead" the nouns they describe; that is, the adjective comes first and the noun follows.

***old* employee** ***loyal* citizen** ***blue* dress** ***thin* person**

Checkup 7. Underline each adjective.

1. Karol wore his red vest with his grey jeans.
2. When you get a new car, will you sell your old truck?
3. Concerned voters should demand an honest election.

Following Adjectives. Most adjectives come before the noun they describe, as in the sentences above. Sometimes, however, adjectives may come after the noun, especially if they are in pairs.

Leading Adjectives: **Our *poor, unlucky* relatives lost their land.**

Following Adjectives: **Our relatives, *poor* and *unlucky,* lost their land.**

Checkup 8. Underline each adjective. Then draw an arrow to the noun it modifies.

1. Her blond hair, long and silky, was her best feature.
2. Young children, eager and excited, gathered flowers.
3. Katie, tense and nervous, awaited her first interview.

ADVERBS

Adverbs give more information about verbs, adjectives, or other adverbs. They tell How? When? Where? How much? or To what degree?

Adverbs often modify verbs, as shown by the arrows below.

We ran *fast.* Ran how? *Fast* tells how.

He came *soon.* Came when? *Soon* tells when.

They moved *out.* Moved where? *Out* tells where.

Adverbs also modify adjectives:

This is an *exceptionally* fine painting. *Exceptionally* tells to what degree the painting is *fine*.

And adverbs also modify other adverbs.

They ran *amazingly fast.* Both *amazingly* and *fast* are adverbs. Ran how? *Fast.* How fast? *Amazingly fast.* The adverb *amazingly* modifies the adverb *fast*.

Here are some of the commonly used adverbs: *very, well, often,* and *soon.* In addition, there are many other adverbs that end in *ly.*

exceptionally	**frequently**	**commonly**
unfortunately	**amazingly**	**quickly**

Checkup 9. Underline each adverb. Then draw an arrow to the verb, adjective, or adverb it modifies.

1. She collects very old dishes.
2. Both girls walked rapidly and arrived early.
3. Although we joked quite often, we sensed a rather negative response.

CONJUNCTIONS

Conjunctions join words or groups of words. They are links that hold the parts of your message together. There are many conjunctions, but the most common ones are:

and **or** **nor** **but** **because** **although** **since** **when**

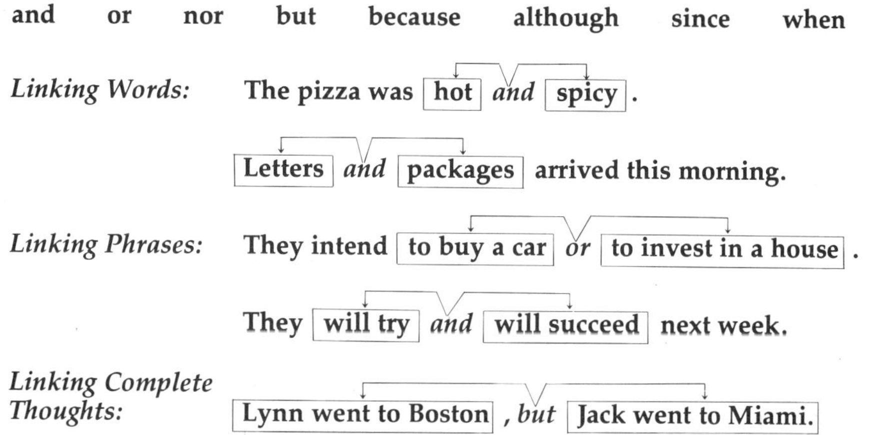

Checkup 10. Underline each conjunction.

1. Spring and summer are not hot or wet in our state.
2. I am lonely since you have been gone.
3. Fall has come, but the trees and lawns are still green.

There are other conjunctions that commonly are used to link complete thoughts: *although, because, since, when, if, whenever,* and others.

He was defeated *because* **he had no support.**
Please let me know *if* **you decide to go.**
Call us *when* **you get to the office.**

PREPOSITIONS

Prepositions lead up to a noun and show some relationship between the noun and the rest of the sentence. Often the relationship deals with "space" or "direction." Here are a few very common prepositions:

from	**in**	**to**	**between**	**of**	**for**	**among**	**over**
behind	**with**	**after**	**by**	**up**	**into**	**before**	**under**

Now let's see how prepositions lead up to nouns:

She sat *between* the two men.

The ball was given *to* the quarterback.

The teacher collected papers *from* the students.

They walked *up* the hill.

Prepositions also lead up to pronouns.

She sat *between* them.
The ball was given *to* him.
The teacher collected students *from* us.

Checkup 11. Underline each preposition and the noun it points to.

1. He came from Minnesota and went to Ohio.
2. They divided the driving among the passengers.
3. This is government of the people, by the people, and for the people.
4. The three of them helped us prepare for the meeting.

These, then, are the seven basic categories of words: nouns, pronouns, verbs, adjectives, adverbs, conjunctions, and prepositions. Each of these seven units will be discussed more fully later. Obviously, the same word may sometimes fall into more than one category, depending upon how you use it in your message. Look at the word *house*, for example.

We own a *house*. *House* is a noun.
We looked at *house* plans. *House* is an adjective describing *plans*.
This building can *house* 100 families. *House* is part of the verb *can house*.

Another example is the word *contract*.

She signed a *contract* with a movie studio. *Contract* is a noun.
The newspaper reported that *contract* talks would begin in April. *Contract* is an adjective; it modifies the noun *talks*.
As you know, metals *contract* when they cool. *Contract* is a verb.

Checkup 12. Identify the italicized words below by writing *noun*, *pronoun*, and so on, in the appropriate space. Follow the example.

0. We *heard* a speech *on* the importance verb ______ preposition ______
   of *effective* communication. adjective ______
1. *Communication* is a two-way process. ______

2. The *sender transmits* a message ______ ______

to a receiver. ______

3. The senders *get* feedback from *their* receivers. ______ ______

4. However, feedback *is* not *always* intentional, ______ ______

and it may not always *be* immediate. ______ ______ ______

5. In addition, not all *important* messages are verbal. ______

6. Some of the most *serious messages*, in fact, are ______ ______

those that *are* written *and* read. ______ ______

7. *Careful and correct* ______ ______ ______

choice of words *is* important. ______ ______

REVIEW QUIZ

Identify the italicized words below by writing *noun*, *pronoun*, and so on, in the space provided. Follow the example.

0. Mr. Boynton *or* Miss Conrad will review this proposal. Conjunction
1. *Alicia*, my supervisor, is an expert in mathematics. ______
2. You and Margo completed the first draft very *fast*. ______
3. Ms. DeBois *hired* an accountant yesterday morning. ______
4. Apparently, *he* was dissatisfied with the results of our survey. ______
5. Ms. Margolies bought an *old* apartment building as an investment. ______
6. The marketing *and* sales departments will be moved to the 15th floor. ______
7. Please place that file cabinet *between* those two desks. ______
8. My supervisors, Harold and *she*, are on vacation this week. ______
9. Give this copy to *John*, please. ______
10. Our company has its headquarters in *Memphis*, Tennessee. ______

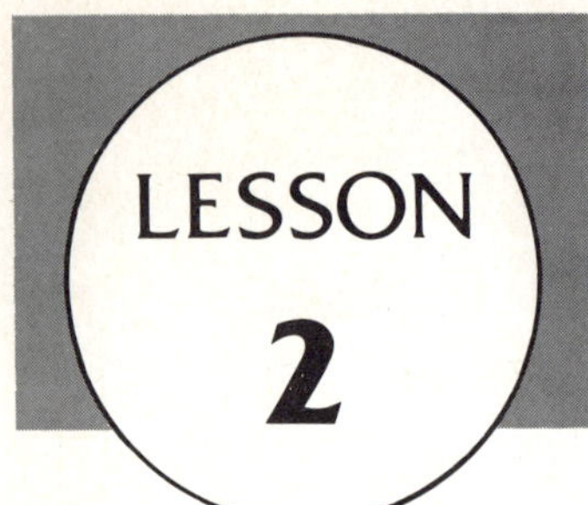

Sentences

Now let's see how you can join these different kinds of words to shape them into messages—into *sentences*. As you will see, sentences have two basic parts: the subject part and the action part.

THE SUBJECT PART

Simple Subjects. Every message is built around a main topic—a special person, thing, or idea that the rest of the words tell about. This topic is called the *subject*. The subject is the person or thing that you're talking about. It is usually a noun or pronoun.

***Craig* won.** ***Wood* will burn.** ***Football* is an exciting game.**
***We* drove downtown.**

Because the subject of each sentence has only one word—*Craig, Wood, Football,* and *We*—it is called the *simple subject*.

Checkup 1. Underline each subject.

1. Chicago is in Illinois.
2. Red was his favorite color.
3. Buses leave from the depot every hour.

Complete Subjects. Sometimes the subject is just one word, as in the examples just given. Other times the subject is a group of words.

***The (player) in the blue shirt* caught the ball.**

***Mr. Case's new (stenographer)* joined our staff Monday.**

The whole group of italicized words is called the *complete subject*. The key circled word in each group is the simple subject. The rest of the words attached to the simple subject give information to tell the reader for sure which subject you're talking about. In the first sentence above, for example, the simple subject is *player*—but which player? The complete subject tells the reader that you're talking about *the player in the blue shirt*, not the player in the white shirt or the one in the yellow shirt. The simple subject of the second sentence is *stenographer*—but which stenographer? The complete subject tells the reader that *Mr. Case's new stenographer* is the topic of the message; this is the person who joined our staff Monday.

Checkup 2. Underline the complete subject and circle the simple subject.

1. The house at the end of the block burned last night.
2. The door to my office is always open.
3. Students who study get good grades.

Now that we've identified the complete subject of a message, let's look at how the other words in the message work.

THE ACTION PART

Every message has two parts. As you saw, the first part is the subject; the second part is called the *action* or *condition* of the subject. All words that are *not* part of the complete subject belong to the action or condition part of the sentence.

Action: **All employees** ***reported for work on time.***
Action: **We** ***refinished the dining room floor.***
Condition: **Our personnel manager** ***is sick.***
Condition: **The fumes from the burner** ***smelled strong.***

Checkup 3. Underline the action or condition part of these sentences.

1. The drawer of my desk is sticky.
2. Pam and Jim went to college in Los Angeles.
3. The report on inventory control looks satisfactory.

Verbs. Do the words *action* and *condition* sound familiar? That's because we used these words when we talked about verbs in the last lesson. The action or condition part of a message always includes a verb. If a message doesn't have a verb, it isn't a message; it is only a topic for a message.

The third car from the end . . . . What about it?
Five managers in our company . . . . What about them?

On the other hand, if it has only the action or condition part of the sentence (the verb and related words), it isn't a message either.

. . . **left early.** Who?
. . . **was spoiled.** Who? or What?

Complete Sentences. The point is this: A complete message must tell (1) who or what the subject is and (2) what the action or condition is. A complete message is called a *sentence.* A sentence can stand alone because it gives the reader a complete thought.

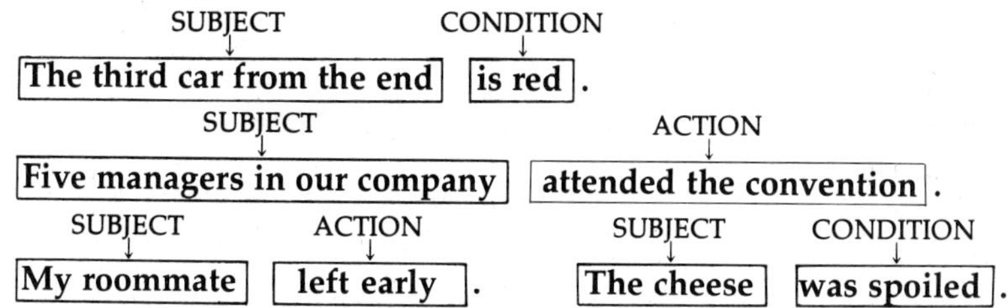

Checkup 4. Underline the complete subject part once and the action or condition part twice.

1. Wool clothing is warmer than cotton.
2. The scissors in my drawer belong to Miss Ames.
3. The two friends went to the movie together.

Unfinished Sentences. Some groups of words look like sentences because they have both a subject and a verb, yet they cannot stand alone if they do not give the reader a complete thought. It often takes more than *just* a subject and a verb to make a sentence. Read the following aloud to see for yourself how each leaves you wondering "Then what?"

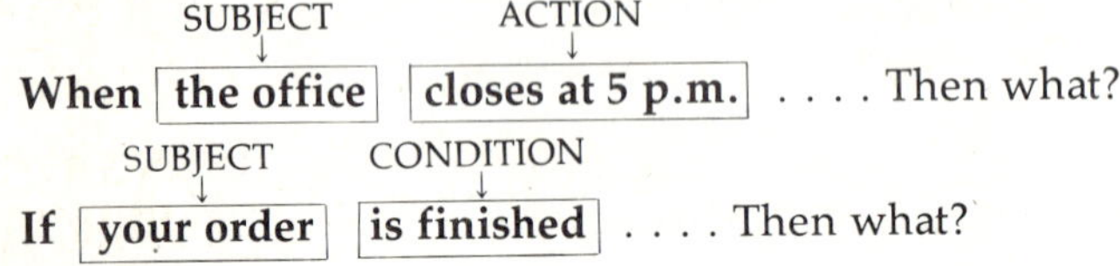

In the unfinished sentences above the words *if* and *when* lead you to expect more to follow; they introduce incomplete thoughts. Thus the examples are only part of a message—a "dependent" group of words that must be connected to a complete thought to make sense. For example:

When the office closes at 5 p.m., we will be able to leave for the airport early. *When the office closes at 5 p.m.* is now connected to a complete thought.

If your order is finished, it will be shipped to you by messenger. *If your order is finished* is now connected to a complete thought.

In these sentences, notice that *we will be able to leave for the airport early* and *it will be shipped to you by messenger* are complete thoughts. Each could stand alone as a sentence.

Checkup 5. Complete the following incomplete thoughts.

1. Because Mrs. Hahn was not at the meeting, ______________________

____

2. Since Vera joined our company last January, ______________________

____

3. Although we left early, ______________________

____

4. When Ms. McNally arrives, ______________________

____

Now indicate whether the following are complete sentences or unfinished sentences. Write *C* for each complete sentence; *U* for each unfinished sentence.

5. Whenever the work becomes very tiresome. 5. ______
6. No one ever knew just what his duties were. 6. ______
7. Since there is no other answer. 7. ______

Compound Subjects. Sometimes two or more nouns or pronouns may be linked by a conjunction to form a *compound subject* and may share the same verb.

SUBJECT ↓ SUBJECT ↓

She and Wilhelmina are friends. Pronoun plus noun.

The cars, the boats, and the planes needed inspection. Three nouns.

My assistant or my manager has the contract file. Two nouns with describing words.

Checkup 6. Underline each part of the compound subject.

1. Saturday, Sunday, and Monday are quiet days.
2. Your parents and my boss are good friends.
3. The job Jake has and the job my brother has are similar.

Compound Verbs. Just as a sentence can have a compound subject, it also can have a compound verb.

VERBS

I *wrote* and *typed* both reports.

VERBS

We *cleaned* and *polished* all the machinery.

In the first sentence above, *reports* is the object of the verbs *wrote* and *typed.* Wrote and typed what? *Reports.* In the second sentence, *machinery* is the object of the verbs *cleaned* and *polished.* Cleaned and polished what? *Machinery.* The *object* is the person or thing that receives the action described by the verb.

Sometimes, each verb has its own object.

VERBS

I *wrote* letters and *typed* reports.

Here, *letters* is the object of *wrote*; and *reports* is the object of *typed.*

VERBS

We *cleaned* the office and *polished* the machinery.

Here, *office* is the object of the verb *cleaned*; and *machinery* is the object of the verb *polished.*

Checkup 7. Underline the compound verbs and their objects, if any. Follow the example.

0. The office crew sorted mail and filed letters.
1. We ate the sandwiches and drank the milk.
2. Our team won the championship and went to the state tournament.
3. My friend is ambitious and will be successful.

USES OF SENTENCES

Sentences are the patterns you use most often in building your messages. But sentences are not all alike. For one thing, sentences differ according to how they are used—according to what you want them to do for you.

Declarative Sentences. Declarative sentences "declare" or make a simple statement. Declarative sentences end with a period.

Today's phone messages are on your desk.
The cycle arrived on Saturday.

Questioning Sentences. Questioning (or interrogative) sentences ask a question and end with a question mark.

When is my first appointment?
Can you fill the order today?

Exclamatory Sentences. Exclamatory sentences show strong feeling or surprise and end with an exclamation point.

You won't believe our offer!
We have good news for you!

Caution: Except in sales material, exclamation points seldom are used in business correspondence. Usually a period is all you need to close a thought.

Checkup 8. Write *D* after declarative sentences, *Q* after questioning sentences, and *E* after exclamatory sentences. Add end punctuation.

1. We need to research the problem 1. ______
2. I don't believe it 2. ______

3. How many copies would you like 3. _______

4. Mrs. Halmy left already, didn't she 4. _______

CAPITALIZATION

You have probably noticed that complete sentences always begin with a capital letter, no matter which end punctuation you use. This is one of the ways you show your reader that you're presenting a complete thought. Each new sentence must begin with a capital letter and end with some sort of punctuation mark, as in the following examples:

When we applied for a job, we were accepted. When my two friends applied for a job, however, they were not accepted. Can you tell me why?

Checkup 9. Add punctuation and capital letters. To capitalize a lowercase letter, underline the letter three times (for example, *american*).

My sister and I went downtown to apply for jobs with an insurance company the jobs had been advertised in the paper did you see the ads why don't you apply too

SPLIT SENTENCES

Be careful not to split a complete sentence into incomplete parts by using extra capital letters or end punctuation where they don't belong.

INCORRECT PUNCTUATION — INCORRECT CAPITALIZATION

Wrong: **They told me. That I could leave.**
Correct: **They told me that I could leave.**

INCORRECT PUNCTUATION — INCORRECT CAPITALIZATION

Wrong: **They wanted to know. When he would be 22.**
Correct: **They wanted to know when he would be 22.**

Checkup 10. Correct each split sentence.

1. Catherine went to an interview. After she left school today. _______________

2. The copies were prepared. On the new machine. _______________

3. We think your way. Is the best way. _______________

4. Please let us know. As soon as Dr. Bergstrom arrives. _______________

Being able to spot and correct unfinished or split sentences is one of the most important lessons in business communication. Before going on to the Section Wrap-Up, review the material in this lesson and try out your skills on Checkup 11.

Checkup 11. The following sentences are unfinished or split. Change or complete these sentences so that they express complete thoughts that can stand alone. Be sure to use correct end punctuation and capital letters.

1. The last piece of paper from the pad. ______________________

____

2. Constant searching for success. Can waste a lifetime. ______________________

____

3. The committee insisted. That the task force meet today. ______________________

____

4. Didn't know how to run the machine. ______________________

____

5. There's a deep ditch. By the fence. At the end of the road. ______________________

____

REVIEW QUIZ

Part 1. Underline the complete subjects once and simple subjects twice. Then circle the action or condition part of each sentence and add end punctuation. Follow the example.

0. This old machine (does not work properly.)
1. The stockholders will meet again tomorrow afternoon
2. My secretary, my supervisor, and I will attend the conference
3. John asked Mrs. Kim for a duplicate copy
4. Nine applicants for the sales position were interviewed yesterday
5. Dr. Andrews or Mrs. Halpern may be able to answer your questions

Part 2. Complete the incomplete thoughts at the top of page 17. Be sure to add capital letters and punctuation. Use three underscores to indicate capitals. Follow this example.

0. although Ms. Wilson ordered 500 copies, we quickly ran out of stock.

____

1. whenever you have time ______________________________

____

2. since we opened our branch office ______________________________

____

3. when we reached San Francisco ______________________________

____

4. because the customer received damaged merchandise ______________________________

____

5. as you probably know ______________________________

____

SECTION 1 WRAP-UP: Units of Communication

The next few pages will wrap up the material in Section 1, "Units of Communication." Look over the reminders and review the goals on page 1 before completing the Spelling Exercise. The sentences you write with the spelling words will show how well you can use what you've learned from this section.

REMINDERS

The following examples are reminders of common, irritating mistakes found in everyday business communication. Do your best to avoid them!

Error: **I wondered if she was competent?**
I asked whether he could come?

These sentences are *not* questions and should not end with a question mark. They are simple declarative statements of something that has been done or thought, and they should end with a period.

Correction: **I wondered if she was competent.**
I asked whether he could come.

Error: **They looked out the window and saw traffic. Stopped for blocks. The shipping department inquired. Where the stock had been sent.**

Be careful not to write unfinished or split sentences! Groups of dependent words that can't stand alone must be tied to a complete thought to make sense.

Correction: **They looked out the window and saw traffic stopped for blocks. The shipping department inquired where the stock had been sent.**

SPELLING EXERCISE

Correct any misspellings in the following list of 15 words. Write your corrections below each word; if a word is correctly spelled, write C below the word. Then for each word write a sentence as described by the instructions. Follow the example.

	WORD	SAMPLE SENTENCE
0.	accurasy	(Sentence with a noun.) Your accuracy is surprising.
	accuracy	
1.	bookeeping	(Sentence with a noun.)
2.	ocassion	(Sentence with a verb.)
3.	expence	(Sentence with a pronoun.)
4.	morgage	(Sentence with an adjective.)
5.	column	(Sentence with an adverb.)
6.	computor	(Sentence with a preposition.)
7.	bankrupcy	(Sentence with a conjunction.)
8.	advice (noun)	(Sentence with a subject.)
9.	advize (verb)	(Sentence with action/condition.)

10. corespondense (Sentence with a compound subject.) ____________

____________ ____

11. licence (Sentence with compound action/condition.) ____________

____________ ____

12. maintainance (Declarative sentence.) ____________

____________ ____

13. propaganda (Questioning sentence.) ____________

____________ ____

14. communication (Exclamatory sentence.) ____________

____________ ____

15. indictment (Unfinished/split sentence.) ____________

____________ ____

Nouns

YOUR GOALS

After finishing this section, you will be able to:

1. Decide which nouns should be capitalized (proper nouns) and which nouns should not be capitalized (common nouns).
2. Properly form the plurals of regular and irregular nouns.
3. Correctly form the possessives of regular and irregular nouns.
4. Correctly spell 15 commonly misspelled words.

LESSON 4 Nouns

Nouns name persons, places, things, or ideas. They're the words that identify what you're talking about. Nouns can be either common or proper.

COMMON NOUNS

A common noun identifies a person, place, thing, or idea that belongs to a general category or group.

street **commissioner** **house**

These words don't identify any special street, commissioner, or house.

PROPER NOUNS

A proper noun, on the other hand, refers to a certain single person, place, thing, or idea. Proper nouns act as titles—they single out an individual item. To make that item special, you capitalize the noun.

Cedar Street **Commissioner Riley** **the White House**

You can see that these words do identify one special item—a specific street, a certain commissioner, and a special house. Thus proper nouns are capitalized.

Checkup 1. Underline each common noun once and each proper noun twice.

1. When Mayor Laramie leaves, we will have new rules.
2. The editor of *Business News* gave a speech at the rally.
3. A committee examined our records and made a decision.

CAPITALIZATION OF PROPER NOUNS

By capitalizing a noun, you make it stand out as a special proper noun. Let's see when you should capitalize nouns—and when you should *not*.

Units of Time. Not all units of time are treated the same. For example, months of the year, days of the week, and holidays are capitalized.

January	**Friday**	**Easter**
April	**Sunday**	**Fourth of July**

On the other hand, seasons of the year and centuries begin with small letters.

summer **spring** **twentieth century**

Geographic Directions. There are similar differences in geographic direction. When referring to points on the compass, do not use a capital letter.

east of Stillwater **turned west** **southern Ohio**

However, references to specific sections of the country or to the people who live there *do* require a capital letter.

the East **a Midwesterner** **South Saint Paul**

Checkup 2. Add capital letters where needed. To capitalize a lowercase letter, underline the letter three times.

1. Our new offices (only six miles east of here) will be open next winter, probably before christmas.
2. Saul Remark, a well-known southerner, visited me on tuesday, august 23.
3. The play was written in the seventeenth century, but it was rewritten by a director from the west coast—from seattle, I believe.

Titles. Most people wonder when words such as *president* and *director* should be capitalized. A few basic rules will help you decide.

When words like *president, secretary,* and *director* are part of a person's formal title and appear just *before* the person's name, they are proper nouns that need a capital letter.

CAPITAL ↓
I spoke to *President* Jan Howe.

CAPITAL ↓
The letter was sent to *Commissioner* Jed Baker.

When these same words *follow* the person's name, they are not part of a formal title. They just rename the person to provide emphasis or to clearly identify the person you've already mentioned. Such a restatement is not capitalized.

NO CAPITAL

Jan Howe, *president* of our group, spoke to us at lunch.

NO CAPITALS

You should ask Francis Magallon, *general manager,* for approval.

When the renaming word comes before the person's name but is not part of a formal title, it is not capitalized and a comma separates the title from the name.

NO CAPITAL COMMA

I spoke to our *president,* Jan Howe.

NO CAPITAL COMMA

The letter was sent to our *councilman,* Jed Baker.

There are, however, some exceptions to these rules. When writing names and titles that stand alone (in inside addresses, signature blocks, envelope addresses, and so on), capitalize both the name and the restatement that follows.

CAPITALS

Ms. Fern Wood, Associate Producer
United Film Industries Inc.
738 Randolph Lane
Los Angeles, CA 90032

CAPITALS

Carl Rupert, Assistant Controller
The McRandall Corporation

Also, as a matter of respect, capitalize all references to the President of the United States.

CAPITAL

The *President* is back in Washington.

CAPITAL

He was the sixth *President* of our country.

Checkup 3. Add capital letters where needed. Write OK if no additional capitals are needed.

1. One of our directors, Myrna Yardley, called a meeting. 1. ________
2. Each new president makes changes in the White House. 2. ________
3. Whenever Alan Fielding, treasurer of the organization, meets with commander Tyson, we expect a disagreement. 3. ________

Government Agencies. Words like *state, federal,* and *government* should not be capitalized unless they are part of a formal title.

NO CAPITAL NO CAPITALS

Our *government* requires us to pay *federal, state,* and local taxes.

NO CAPITAL NO CAPITAL

The *state,* rather than the *city,* should pay for repair of the bridge.

But notice the capitals when these words are part of a formal title.

CAPITAL CAPITAL

The *State* Planning Agency and the *Federal* Trade Commission were represented.

CAPITAL CAPITAL

The *Federal* Bureau of Investigation and the *County* Commission on Crime will check the records.

Checkup 4. Add capital letters where needed.

1. The complaint was signed by the district attorney for New York City.
2. Some people consider federal welfare programs essential.
3. Many employees of the state department of education are paid with funds from the federal government.

These few rules will help you decide whether or not you should use capital letters. However, they don't provide *all* the answers. You'll need to use an up-to-date dictionary to decide about words in forms of address (*Reverend, the Honorable,* and so on), about trade names (*Touch-Tone dialing* and *Scotch tape*), and about special words (such as *Geiger counter, Cornish hen,* or *Roman Catholic*). If you aren't sure if a word should be capitalized, look it up!

Checkup 5. Underline all nouns; then correct the capitalization of each sentence. To capitalize a lowercase letter, underline the letter three times. To change a capital letter to lowercase, draw a line through the letter (for example, *the Boys*).

0. dayton's is moving its Branch Office to new york city in april.
1. This book on Washington, our first president, is an excellent Biography.
2. The Army headed West into Federal territory.
3. Marie Kelly, Secretary-Treasurer of the Camera Club, was awarded a State scholarship.
4. The Report was sent to one of our personnel Offices.
5. Representatives from the State department of education, the federal bureau of investigation, and School District 461 will testify.
6. Repairers from one of the Maintenance Departments will check the switches and wires before the Office closes for the Weekend.
7. The young man bought a copy of the *wall street journal,* as well as the latest issue of *Reader's Treat.*

8. The TV movie about former president nixon was broadcast throughout the Country, as well as in Europe.

USES OF NOUNS

We said in the last lesson that nouns are subjects of sentences—the topics of our messages. But you mustn't think that all nouns are automatically subjects or "doers of the action." Nouns can do more than that. They also can be used as objects of verbs or objects of prepositions.

As Subjects of Sentences. Just as a review, here's another example of a noun as subject of a sentence. (This subject happens to be a capitalized proper noun.)

SUBJECT
↓
***Fred* opened an appliance store.**

As Objects of Verbs. As the object of a verb, a noun *receives* the action of the verb. In other words, the object has something done to it.

Caroline opened the *mail*.

The noun *mail* is the object of the verb *opened*. Opened what? *Opened the mail*. *Mail* receives the action of the verb *opened*. *Caroline*, of course, is the subject of the sentence, the doer of the action.

The student erased his *mistake*.

The noun *mistake* is the object of the verb *erased*. *Mistake* is a noun—it is the thing that receives the action of the verb *erased*. Erased what? *Mistake*. The subject of the sentence—the doer of the action—is *the student*.

Checkup 6. Circle the object of the verb. (***Hint:*** Each verb is in *italics*.)

1. One of the trainees *answered* the phone.
2. The office staff *signed* a petition.
3. Several other people *considered* your suggestion.

As Objects of Prepositions. Another kind of noun-object is the object of a preposition. As we noted in the last lesson, a preposition leads up to or prepares the way for the noun that follows. Together, the preposition and the noun form a *prepositional phrase*.

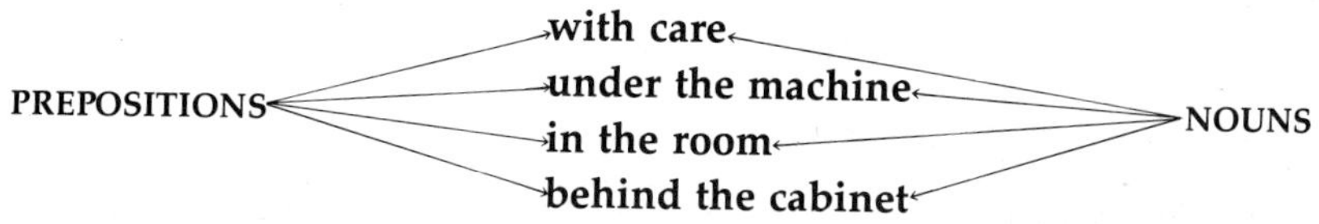

The noun in each phrase on page 25 is the object of the preposition.

PREPOSITION OBJECT OF PREPOSITION

We went to the *meeting.*

The preposition *to* prepares the way for *meeting,* linking it to the rest of the sentence to show where we went.

PREPOSITION OBJECT OF PREPOSITION

The schedule was rearranged for the *employees.*

For leads up to its object, *employees,* to give you the rest of the thought—to tell you for whom the schedule was rearranged.

Checkup 7. Circle each object of the preposition. (***Hint:*** Each preposition is in *italics*.)

1. Ask her to come *into* my office.
2. Our department received a memo *from* Ralph.
3. The magazine was filled *with* good ideas.

As Restatements. Another way you can use a noun is to repeat or restate another noun. By using a restatement, you make the first noun clearer, more emphatic. What you're really doing is naming the person, place, thing, or idea twice—but in different words.

Remember: Restatements are generally separated from the nouns they rename with commas.

RESTATEMENT

Mrs. Prigge, our *bookkeeper,* will help you with your account.

Bookkeeper restates *Mrs. Prigge* in different words in order to clearly identify the person you're talking about. Note that two commas are used to separate the restatement from the rest of the sentence.

RESTATEMENT

I traveled to my favorite city, *New York.*

New York is a restatement of the noun it follows. *New York* is a restatement of *my favorite city;* they are different words for the same place.

Checkup 8. Underline each restatement. Then draw an arrow to the noun it renames.

1. His new title, manager, was added to his nameplate.
2. You should contact two people, Ed and Sharon.
3. The second publication, a magazine, was also ordered.
4. Only one person, Carol Ducey, has the authority to approve these expenses.

As Adjectives. You know from Lesson 1 that adjectives describe nouns or pronouns. You also can use a noun as an adjective. In this case, one noun simply describes another noun.

ADJECTIVE NOUN

The *typewriter* ribbons have been ordered.

Typewriter often is used alone as a noun, but here it is used to describe *ribbons.* It tells what kinds of ribbons have been ordered. In this case, therefore, *typewriter* is a noun-adjective.

ADJECTIVE NOUN

None of the applicants belonged to the *company* club.

Company is often used as a noun, but here it describes and identifies the next noun, *club.* It tells which club is being discussed. *Company,* therefore, is a noun-adjective.

Checkup 9. Underline each noun-adjective. Then draw an arrow to the noun it describes.

1. Her secretary makes all of her travel arrangements.
2. Did you receive a confirmation of my hotel reservation?
3. I have a different morning assignment each day.

Now let's put together what you've learned about nouns so far.

Checkup 10. In the following sentences, (1) underline all common nouns and (2) circle all proper nouns. Then (3) show how each noun is used by writing *S* above subjects, *OV* above objects of verbs, *OP* above objects of prepositions, *R* above restatements, and *AJ* above adjectives (including noun-adjectives). Follow the example.

0. Their children (S), (Raphael and Anne) (R), deposited the money (OV) in the bank (OP).
1. Mr. Roth, our chairman, is investigating discrimination cases for the state government.
2. The company gave a watch to Ms. Gomez for her anniversary.
3. Many cartons of papers were left in the hall.
4. Yes, the bank will be open for Saturday business.
5. Jupiter, the largest planet, will be visited soon.
6. Frequent movies and plays delighted the travelers.
7. The men carried the packages on their shoulders.
8. Rocks and rubbish, piled in a heap, marked the spot.

REVIEW QUIZ

Correct any errors in capitalization in the following sentences. Follow the example for indicating your corrections. Write C if a sentence is correct as given.

0. members of the union appealed to mr. H. R. Silkow, one of the Union Representatives.
1. Several Members of our committee argued about Federal and State funds.
2. Maude has already reserved a Conference Room for next thursday's meeting, and she has invited mayor Schwartz to join us.
3. Anna Benson, a Public Relations expert, is a former Member of the white house press staff.
4. On march 1, our Company will celebrate its Twenty-Fifth Anniversary.
5. The President of our corporation assigned several people to a Special Committee for the purpose of studying Consumers' attitudes.
6. the supervisor of our department, helen b. wickers, taught english for several years before she joined our Firm.
7. We are now interviewing Candidates for six positions; the Candidates were referred to us by an Employment Agency.
8. Ms. Hillebrand has written three Children's Books, all of which have been Best-Sellers.
9. Perhaps Dr. DeMarco, who has been on our Staff for several years, can help us develop some new Procedures for handling Marketing Research projects.
10. Anthony Winston was recently promoted to a Management Position with one of our Branch Offices.

LESSON 5

Plurals of Nouns

Nouns can be either singular or plural. *Singular* means "single"—just one. Singular nouns name *one* person, place, thing, or idea. *Plural* means "two or more." Plural nouns tell the reader you're talking about *more* than one item.

REGULAR PLURALS

We know from using our language that most nouns are made plural by simply adding an *s* to the singular noun.

car/cars **bridge/bridges** **letter/letters** **check/checks**

Adding *s* works for many nouns in our language, but it does not work for all of them. The rest of this lesson is concerned with special plurals.

SPECIAL PLURALS

Some nouns form their plurals in a special way.

Nouns Ending in *S, X, Z, CH, SH.* Plurals for nouns ending in *s, x, z, ch,* and *sh* require an *es* ending in order to make them easier to pronounce. You can hear the *es* sound at the end of these plurals when you pronounce them. Say these pairs aloud and listen to the *es* sound.

boss/boss*es* **box/box*es*** **buzz/buzz*es*** **lunch/lunch*es*** **wish/wish*es***

Checkup 1. Form plurals of the following nouns.

1. lash ______________ 3. church ______________ 5. mess ______________
2. miss ______________ 4. pass ______________ 6. mix ______________

Nouns Ending in *Y*. Another special group includes singular nouns ending in *y*. These are a little tricky because their plurals depend on the letter that comes just before the final *y*. If a vowel (*a, e, i, o, u*) comes just before the *y*, form the plural by simply adding an *s*.

VOWEL ↓ **turkey/turkeys** VOWEL ↓ **holiday/holidays**

For nouns with *no vowel* just before the *y*, form the plural by changing the *y* to *i* and adding *es*.

NO VOWEL ↓ **baby/bab*ies*** (*y* TO *i*) NO VOWEL ↓ **city/cit*ies*** (*y* TO *i*)

Let's go over these rules once more: (1) The *y* is changed to *i* and (2) *es* is added only if a letter *other* than a vowel comes just before the final *y*.

Checkup 2. Form plurals of the following nouns.

1. candy ______________ 3. jelly ______________ 5. country ______________
2. day ______________ 4. lady ______________ 6. cowboy ______________

Nouns Ending in *O*. Nouns that end in *o* also may have different plural forms. As with *y*-ending nouns, you have to look at the letter that comes just before the ending. If a vowel (*a, e, i, o, u*) comes just before the final *o*, just add an *s* to form the plural.

VOWEL ↓ **studio/studios** VOWEL ↓ **folio/folios**

The vowel before the final *o* makes the word regular, like the majority of nouns in our language, so you just add an *s* to make it plural.

But when there is *no* vowel before the final *o*, the plural form usually requires an *es*.

NO VOWEL ↓ **tomato/tomato*es*** NO VOWEL ↓ **hero/hero*es***

Notice the above rule says that you usually add *es* when a letter other than a vowel comes before the final *o*. There are exceptions, however.

Musical Terms. Most musical terms are exceptions to the rule. They don't use an *es* ending, no matter what letter comes before the final *o*.

NO VOWEL ↓	NO VOWEL ↓	NO VOWEL ↓
piano/pianos	**solo/solos**	**cello/cellos**
↑ NO *e*!	↑ NO *e*!	↑ NO *e*!

Be sure to check your dictionary for plurals of seldom-used *o*-ending words.

Checkup 3. Form plurals of the following nouns.

1. radio ____________
2. halo ____________
3. trio ____________
4. concerto ____________
5. soprano ____________
6. rodeo ____________

Nouns Ending in *F* or *FE*. Plurals of most nouns ending in *f* or *fe* are regular; that is, they become plural by simply adding an *s*.

roof/roofs **safe/safes**

However, this group does include a number of words that change their patterns when they become plural. In these cases, the *f* is changed to *v* before the plural ending is added.

f TO *v* ↓	*f* TO *v* ↓
leaf/leaves	**life/lives**

Notice that *es* is added if the word doesn't end in *e*: *leaf/leaves* and *sheaf/sheaves*. Words ending in *fe* require only *s*: *life/lives* and *knife/knives*. Be sure to check your dictionary if you aren't sure of a spelling!

Checkup 4. Form plurals of the following nouns.

1. wolf ____________
2. thief ____________
3. spoof ____________
4. elf ____________
5. wife ____________
6. chief ____________

Irregular Plurals. A few common words change their patterns even more when becoming plurals.

woman/women **man/men** **child/children**

Although there is no rule covering all irregular plurals, you already are familiar with the form of most irregulars, so they will cause little trouble.

Compound Nouns. Most of the plurals we have formed so far have been plurals of single words. Now let's look at the plural forms of compound nouns; that is, nouns that consist of two or more words (for example, *timekeeper* and *labor union*).

Most compound nouns that are written as one word are treated just as if they were ordinary, single-word nouns. Add the plural form to the end of the word in the "usual" way:

drugstore/drugstores **businesswoman/businesswomen**
bookshelf/bookshelves

On the other hand, plurals of compound nouns that are written as two separate words or that are tied together with a hyphen usually are formed by adding the plural ending to *the most important word* in the compound.

sister-in-law/sisters-in-law **runner-up/runners-up**
editor in chief/editors in chief **vice president/vice presidents**

Caution: Because there are so many variations, the safest way to determine plurals for unfamiliar compounds is to consult your dictionary. One exception to the rules for compounds is *passerby/passersby* (the first unit is made plural).

Nouns With Only One Form. Some nouns have only one form for both singular and plural. Most of these nouns are not commonly used in business correspondence.

series/series **corps/corps**
moose/moose **salmon/salmon**
deer/deer **sheep/sheep**

Checkup 5. Form plurals of the following nouns.

1. jack-of-all-trades ______ 3. sheep ______ 5. pocketknife ______
2. grandchild ______ 4. typewriter ______ 6. court-martial ______

PLURALS OF NAMES

In the lesson on capitalization we found that proper nouns (names) are made special by using capital letters. However, we do not do anything special to form the plurals of names. We generally just add *s* or *es* as with any other word.

Joseph/two Josephs **Trish/two Trishes**

The only rule to remember is that the pattern of the name is never changed in making the plural, no matter how the name is spelled.

Mr. and Mrs. Freeman/the Freemans *(not: the Freemen)*
Mr. and Mrs. Henry/the Henrys *(not: the Henries)*

Checkup 6. Form plurals of the following proper nouns.

1. Mary ______ 3. Frank Carlos ______ 5. Florence ______
2. Alf ______ 4. Harold ______ 6. Anthony ______

PLURALS OF COURTESY TITLES

Courtesy titles have special plural forms.

1. The plural of *Mr.* is *Messrs.* (*Mr.* and *Messrs.* are always abbreviated.)

   ***Mr.* Jackson, *Mr.* Croup, and *Mr.* Thomas**
   ***But: Messrs.* Jackson, Croup, and Thomas**

2. The usual plural of *Mrs.* is *Mesdames* (frequently abbreviated *Mmes.*).

   ***Mrs.* Curry, *Mrs.* Ashland, and *Mrs.* Sunnova**
   ***But: Mesdames* Curry, Ashland, and Sunnova**
   ***Or: Mmes.* Curry, Ashland, and Sunnova**

3. The plural of *Miss* is *Misses.* (It is not an abbreviation; thus no period is needed.)

   ***Miss* Ronson and *Miss* Peters**
   ***But: Misses* Ronson and Peters**

4. The usual plural of *Ms.* is *Mss.* (These courtesy titles do *not* indicate marital status of women and are often used as counterparts to *Mrs.* and *Mmes.*)

   ***Ms.* Rothenstein and *Ms.* Hatch**
   ***But: Mss.* Rothenstein and Hatch**

Checkup 7. Write one plural courtesy title to replace all the individual courtesy titles below. Rewrite the complete answer.

1. Mr. Catlin, Mr. Rugby, Mr. Browne, and Mr. Olsen

   Or: ______________________________

2. Mrs. Catlin, Mrs. Rugby, Mrs. Browne, and Mrs. Olsen

   Or: ______________________________

3. Miss Catlin, Miss Rugby, Miss Browne, and Miss Olsen

   Or: ______________________________

4. Ms. Catlin, Ms. Rugby, Ms. Browne, and Ms. Olsen

   Or: ______________________________

PLURALS OF FOREIGN NOUNS

We need to mention one other group of nouns. These are the words that have been borrowed from foreign languages. Many of these nouns form their plurals by changing the word ending. In addition, a number of them have both a foreign and an English form. A few common examples are given here and in the spelling exercise of this section. For seldom-used words the surest reference is—again—an up-to-date dictionary.

alumnus (graduate, especially male)/**alumni** (male or both sexes)
alumna (female graduate)/**alumnae**

matrix/matrices	**crisis/crises**	**vertebra/vertebrae**
criterion/criteria or **criterions**	**curriculum/curricula** (preferred) or **curriculums**	

And that's all you need to know about making plurals. Are you ready for a review quiz?

REVIEW QUIZ

Write the plural form of each noun.

	SINGULAR			SINGULAR	
1.	rule	______	16.	attorney	______
2.	key	______	17.	Mr. Jones	______
3.	ruby	______	18.	Ms. Smythe	______
4.	patio	______	19.	Mrs. Parry	______
5.	wife	______	20.	criterion	______
6.	piano	______	21.	community	______
7.	editor in chief	______	22.	radio	______
8.	Miss	______	23.	bulletin board	______
9.	Mrs.	______	24.	city	______
10.	Ms.	______	25.	son-in-law	______
11.	Mr.	______	26.	Joseph	______
12.	crisis	______	27.	Ms. Bench	______
13.	go-between	______	28.	life	______
14.	box	______	29.	tax	______
15.	alumnus	______	30.	territory	______

LESSON 6

Possessives of Nouns

Before we discuss the forms and uses of possessive nouns, let's quickly review what you've learned about nouns so far. A noun names something. To make it a special proper noun, you add capital letters. To make it plural, you usually add an *s* or an *es* to the end of the word. Now, what do you do to the pattern of the noun if you want to show possession, ownership, or origin? Fortunately, there is a special punctuation mark to indicate possession—the apostrophe.

SINGULAR POSSESSIVES

The General Rule. To form the possessive of singular nouns, add an apostrophe plus *s*.

SINGULAR	SINGULAR POSSESSIVE	SINGULAR	SINGULAR POSSESSIVE
friend	**friend's help**	**manager**	**manager's goals**
typist	**typist's skill**	**boss**	**boss's office**
class	**class's project**	**Mary**	**Mary's car**
Ms. Cohen	**Ms. Cohen's commission**	**Mr. Lloyd**	**Mr. Lloyd's suggestion**
Al Schwartz	**Al Schwartz's opinion**	**Ben Marx**	**Ben Marx's friend**

Checkup 1. Fill in the correct possessive form of each of the following nouns.

	SINGULAR	SINGULAR POSSESSIVE
1.	actress	______________ role
2.	driver	______________ route
3.	Carla	______________ mother
4.	secretary	______________ promotion
5.	Anthony	______________ raise
6.	team	______________ record
7.	company	______________ earnings
8.	employee	______________ timecard
9.	Mr. Blatz	______________ error
10.	Ross	______________ hobby

The Exceptions. There are a few exceptions to the "apostrophe plus *s*" rule for forming the possessives of singular nouns, and you should be aware of these exceptions. Some proper names that end in *s* take only an apostrophe to form their possessives; others take the apostrophe plus *s*.

APOSTROPHE ONLY	APOSTROPHE PLUS *s*
Mr. Williams' appointment	**Mr. Harris's office**
Mrs. Hastings' stocks	**Mrs. Cross's comments**
Mrs. Onassis' picture	**Dr. Ross's schedule**

You can tell whether to add (1) the apostrophe only or (2) the apostrophe plus *s* by the pronunciation of the possessive form. Pronounce the possessive to yourself before writing it. If you hear an extra "es" sound when you say the possessive, add the apostrophe plus *s*. (The *s* stands for the extra syllable.) If adding the extra syllable sounds awkward when you say the word, then add only the apostrophe.

In the examples above, listen for the pronunciation that sounds most natural. *Williams's appointment* would sound awkward; it is better to say *Williams' appoint-*

ment. Hastings's stocks and *Onassis's picture* also would sound awkward; it is better to say *Hastings' stocks* and *Onassis' picture*. Notice that many proper names ending in *s* and having two or more syllables generally sound better without the extra "es" sound.

Checkup 2. Fill in the correct possessive form of each of the following names.

1. Mr. Grimes — Mr. ______________ business
2. Les — ______________ new car
3. Ms. McNaries — Ms. ______________ promotion
4. Jack Walters — Jack ______________ friend
5. Dr. Von Klutz — Dr. Von ______________ discovery
6. Frances Jeffries — Frances ______________ election

PLURAL POSSESSIVES

Plural Nouns Ending in *S*. Plural nouns that end in *s* simply add an apostrophe to form their possessives. (Note that no new "es" sound is added; therefore, no *s* is added after the apostrophe.)

APOSTROPHE ONLY — **the boys' team**　　APOSTROPHE ONLY — **the executives' reasons**

Plural Nouns Not Ending in *S*. Plurals that don't end in *s* need an apostrophe plus *s* to show possession. (Note that a new "es" sound is added; therefore, an *s* must be added after the apostrophe.)

APOSTROPHE PLUS *s* — **men's suggestions**　　APOSTROPHE PLUS *s* — **children's books**

Checkup 3. Form possessives of the following plural nouns.

1. boys ______________　2. bosses ______________　3. oxen ______________

Common Errors. When you form the possessive of plural nouns, be sure you don't confuse the plural possessive with the singular possessive for the same word. Here's a common error:

Both *company's* presidents were at the meeting.

Company's sounds correct, but it's wrong. It should be *companies'*, because a plural is obviously needed. You can form such possessives correctly by remembering this rule: If a plural possessive is needed, make the word plural first; then make it possessive. *Never* tack on the possessive marker (the apostrophe *or* the apostrophe plus *s*) until you have made the word plural. You know that many words will change their patterns as they become plural. By first making the word plural, you will be sure to add the possessive to the final plural form.

When you've formed the plural of a word, notice whether it already ends in *s*. If it does, just add an apostrophe. If it does not, add an apostrophe plus *s*. Let's look at the possessive forms of several singular and plural words.

SINGULAR	SINGULAR POSSESSIVE	PLURAL	PLURAL POSSESSIVE
grandchild	**grandchild's toys**	**grandchildren**	**grandchildren's toys**
↑ NO *s*	↑ NEEDS *s*	↑ NO *s*	↑ NEEDS *s*

Since the plural *grandchildren* is a plural that does not end in *s*, the possessive form needs *both* an apostrophe *and* an *s*.

Mr. Bass	**Mr. Bass's car**	**the Basses**	**the Basses' car**
↑ *s*-ENDING	↑ APOSTROPHE PLUS *s*	↑ *s*-ENDING	↑ APOSTROPHE ONLY

Since *Basses* is a plural that does end in *s*, only an apostrophe is added.

company	**company's stock**	**companies**	**companies' stock**
↑ NO *s*	↑ APOSTROPHE PLUS *s*	↑ *s*-ENDING	↑ APOSTROPHE ONLY

Again, since *companies* is a plural that does end in *s*, only an apostrophe is needed for the plural possessive.

Remember: Form the plural of the word first. Then notice whether it already ends in *s*. If so, add an apostrophe alone. If not, you need an apostrophe plus *s*.

Checkup 4. For each of the following singular nouns, form the singular possessive, the plural, and the plural possessive. Use your dictionary, if necessary. An example is given.

	SINGULAR	SINGULAR POSSESSIVE	PLURAL	PLURAL POSSESSIVE
0.	duck	duck's	ducks	ducks'
1.	chief	________	________	________
2.	alumna	________	________	________
3.	business	________	________	________
4.	company	________	________	________
5.	chairperson	________	________	________
6.	church	________	________	________
7.	lady	________	________	________
8.	gentleman	________	________	________
9.	sheep	________	________	________
10.	child	________	________	________
11.	Williams	________	________	________

	SINGULAR	SINGULAR POSSESSIVE	PLURAL	PLURAL POSSESSIVE
12.	Walsh	______	______	______
13.	Mary	______	______	______
14.	Marie	______	______	______
15.	director	______	______	______
16.	family	______	______	______
17.	committee	______	______	______
18.	woman	______	______	______
19.	Mr. Harris	______	______	______
20.	executive	______	______	______

JOINT OWNERSHIP

You know that possessives can show ownership by one person.

Jack *Smith's* car

You also know that possessives can show ownership by one *group* of people.

the *Smiths'* car

Sometimes, rather than list the Smiths collectively, you may decide to list them individually. Assume, for example, that Jack and Karen own one car. How could you show this joint ownership? Which would you say?

Jack's and Karen's car
or
Jack and Karen's car

The rule is simple. If two or more people own something jointly, then use *one* possessive marker on the last name listed—not on each of the names listed.

ONE POSSESSIVE MARKER

Joint Possession: **Jack and Karen's car uses diesel fuel.**

ONE POSSESSIVE MARKER

Cheryl and Stan's wedding was spectacular.

Separate possession, however, requires separate possessive markers—one for each name listed:

SEPARATE POSSESSIVE MARKERS

Separate Possession: **Cindy's and Jack's assignments were finished on time.**

SEPARATE POSSESSIVE MARKERS

The Joneses' and the Merrils' homes are both for sale.

Checkup 5. Decide if the following italicized phrases show joint ownership. Then add one or two possessive markers, as required. Follow the example.

0. *Larry*'s *and Paul*'s schools are in the same town.
1. *Fromme and Mace* new store is in the downtown area.
2. She doesn't know whether she will accept *Curl and Helen invitation*.
3. *Bill and Jacob* jobs are very similar.
4. Did you know that *Carla and Rose* husbands are both musicians?
5. According to the report, *Baker & Tyler* latest product should be a best-seller.
6. *Houston and Fort Worth* mayors are scheduled to speak at the dinner tonight.

REVIEW QUIZ

For each of the following singular nouns, write the singular possessive, the plural, and the plural possessive. Follow the example.

	SINGULAR	SINGULAR POSSESSIVE	PLURAL	PLURAL POSSESSIVE
0.	teacher	teacher's	teachers	teachers'
1.	family			
2.	Mr. Bertrand			
3.	woman			
4.	grandchild			
5.	community			

	SINGULAR	SINGULAR POSSESSIVE	PLURAL	PLURAL POSSESSIVE
6.	baby	________	________	________
7.	instructor	________	________	________
8.	agency	________	________	________
9.	mother-in-law	________	________	________
10.	Harry	________	________	________
11.	Mrs. Rubin	________	________	________
12.	Miss Jones	________	________	________
13.	memo	________	________	________
14.	company	________	________	________
15.	government	________	________	________

SECTION 2 WRAP-UP: Nouns

The wrap-up suggestions and exercises will help you review the lessons on nouns. Reread the lessons if you have questions.

COMMON NOUN ERRORS

The following statements are reminders of common, irritating mistakes in the use of nouns. Do your best to avoid these errors!

Error: **The menu included baked *potatos*. She did not want *tomatos* on her salad.**

When an *o*-ending word has no vowel just before the final *o*, the plural usually requires an *es*, not just *s*. (There are exceptions, however, so use your dictionary.)

Correction: **The menu included baked potato*es*. She did not want tomato*es*.**

Error: **When I am in Chicago next fall, I plan to visit that *cities'* museums.**

This form would be correct only if you were talking about the museums of several cities. Since only one city is involved, the noun *city* should not be made plural (*cities*) before the possessive ending is added.

Correction: **When I am in Chicago next fall, I plan to visit that *city's* museums.**

Error: **When we visited the *Jones',* we learned that the *Marshall's* and the *Burns'* are selling their homes.**

Plurals are not formed by adding apostrophes! Plurals are made by adding *s* or *es.* Don't confuse possessives (which use apostrophes) with plurals (which do not)! When you want to make a plural possessive, form the plural of the word first; then make it possessive.

Correction: **When we visited the *Joneses,* we learned that the *Marshalls* and the *Burnses* are selling their homes.** (These are simple plurals.)

SPELLING EXERCISE

Use your dictionary to correct all misspellings in the following list of plural nouns. Then give the singular form for each word. Follow the example. Write *C* in the Correction column if a word is a correctly spelled plural.

	PLURAL	CORRECTION	SINGULAR
0.	branchs	branches	branch
1.	hypothises		
2.	brother-in-laws		
3.	potatos		
4.	attornies		
5.	emfasis		
6.	alumni		
7.	criterea		
8.	perenthases		
9.	burreaus		
10.	auditors		
11.	sargeants		
12.	lieutenents		
13.	biographies		

PLURAL	CORRECTION	SINGULAR
14. agendaes	__________	__________
15. campuses	__________	__________
16. sheeps	__________	__________
17. the Freemans	__________	__________
18. Mrs. Manley's	__________	__________
19. Messrs. Raymond	__________	__________
20. facilitys	__________	__________
21. lifes	__________	__________
22. radioes	__________	__________
23. bookshelfs	__________	__________
24. studios	__________	__________
25. wishs	__________	__________

One final spelling hint: Sometimes you will find it hard to decide whether a compound word should be spelled as one word, as two separate words, or as a hyphened word. The first reference is your dictionary. If you don't find the word there, use the following guidelines:

1. Write unlisted compound nouns as two words (for example, *training ground*).
2. Write unlisted compound verbs with a hyphen (for example, *heat-treat*).
3. Write unlisted compound adjectives with a hyphen (for example, *new-fallen snow*).

Verbs

YOUR GOALS

After finishing this section, you will be able to:

1. Identify action verbs, linking verbs, and verb phrases.
2. Form past tenses, past participles, and present participles from basic verbs.
3. Use the proper verb form and the correct helping verb to show different time relationships.
4. Master the most common troublesome verbs.
5. Correctly spell 15 commonly misspelled verbs.

LESSON 8 Verbs

As you remember, nouns are the words that tell what your messages are about. But nouns tell only half the story. In order to GO anywhere or DO anything, a noun needs help. Even to BE anything, your word pattern needs power, in this case, the power of a verb.

A verb is the part of a sentence that shows action or condition of the subject. Without a verb, the subject would hang in midair and never communicate a message. Look at an example:

The player . . . the ball, and the team . . . .

Without any verbs, the reader will not understand the message. What did the player do with the ball? Hit it? Miss it? Catch it? Throw it? What did the team do? Win? Lose? Cheer? Go home? The reader has no way of knowing what happened.

Obviously, verbs are very important words—they can make your message sing or shout or move or stop. In fact, verbs can make your message do anything you want it to. To write effective sentences you need to know the different kinds of verbs and what each can do.

ACTION VERBS

Let's start with the simplest kind of verb—the action verb, the one that shows that something is happening.

Object Verbs. Many action verbs have objects. The object is the receiver or the result of the action.

VERB ↓ OBJECT ↓

The mail carrier *delivers* packages. *Packages* is the object; it receives the action of the verb *delivers.*

VERB ↓ OBJECT ↓

Jeannie *called* Mary. *Mary* is the object; she received the action of *called.*

In each example, you can find the object by locating the verb and then asking yourself "what?" or "whom?" Delivers what? *Packages.* Called whom? *Mary.* Saying "what?" or "whom?" after the verb will help you to identify the object quickly.

A verb may have more than one object:

VERB OBJECTS

Our staff *donated* time and money. Here, both *time* and *money* are objects. Donated what? *Time and money.*

VERB OBJECTS

They *hired* two managers, one bookkeeper, and one secretary. Hired whom? *Managers, bookkeeper, secretary.*

An object may have more than one verb:

VERBS OBJECT

The custodian *washed* and *polished* the floor. Washed and polished what? *Floor.*

Checkup 1. Underline each verb and circle its object or objects.

1. Ms. Cardici dictated four letters and two memos this morning.
2. We exchanged gifts at the office party.
3. Each staff member wrote and submitted a proposal.
4. The customer returned the merchandise.

No-Object Verbs. Some action verbs are complete in themselves. They do not have objects; they do not show a receiver or result of the action. These words are called *no-object verbs.*

VERB VERB VERB

The custodian finally *arrived.* Then Nate *rose* and *left.* There is no receiver of the action performed by the custodian or by Nate. In each sentence, the action just happens. The verbs *arrived, rose,* and *left* have no objects.

Checkup 2. Underline each no-object verb.

1. All three telephones rang at once.
2. Last Tuesday the shipping clerk resigned.
3. The store opens at 6 a.m. each day.

LINKING VERBS

Another kind of verb is called a *linking verb,* because it links parts of the sentence but does not really show action. Instead, it shows the condition, or state of being, of the subject. The most common of the linking verbs is *be,* with all its forms (*is, am, are, was, were, be, been,* and *being*).

I *am* unemployed.
You *were* correct.

They *will be* sorry.
Carl *was* in Chicago.

She *would have been* proud.
This equipment *is* expensive.

In addition to *be* and its forms, several other linking verbs are commonly used to show the condition of the subject without showing action.

look	**become**	**sound**	**appear**	**remain**
feel	**taste**	**seem**	**smell**	**grow**

The contract *seems* legal. **The clerk *looks* angry.**

You can tell these words are being used as linking verbs because they could be replaced by the linking verb *is* without destroying the sense of the sentence.

Linking: **The noise *sounds* unbearable.** It *is* unbearable.
She *feels* ill. She *is* ill.
The food *tastes* spicy. It *is* spicy.

The linking verbs above could be replaced by *is* without changing the meaning of the message. But some linking verbs also can be action verbs with objects.

Action: **The operator *sounds* the alarm when a fire occurs.** Sounds what? *Alarm* is the object.
She *feels* the baby's forehead to check for fever. Feels what? *Forehead.*
He *tastes* the food for flavor. Tastes what? *Food.*

The verbs above are action verbs and need objects; they cannot logically be replaced by *is.*

Checkup 3. Underline each linking verb. Circle each action verb.

1. The workload becomes heavier each year.
2. I am happy in my job, but Julius is dissatisfied.
3. George grows the flowers himself.

VERB PHRASES

Verbs don't always work alone. Sometimes they team up to form *verb phrases.*

John ***has been transferred.*** **In July he** ***will be moving*** **to Colorado.** *Has been transferred* and *will be moving* are verb phrases.

A verb phrase is a main verb plus one or more helping verbs. The main verb is *always* the last verb in the phrase. The main verb may be an action verb, or it may be a linking verb.

Except for the last verb (the main verb), all the verbs in a verb phrase are called *helpers.* In the following verb phrases, note that the main verb, the last verb, is in italics:

am ***going***	**have been** ***invited***
was ***looking***	**did** ***ask***
were ***asking***	**do** ***type***
will be ***writing***	**should have been** ***corrected***
might be ***promoted***	**must have been** ***lost***

Note, too, that in questions one of the helpers is usually separated from the rest of the verb phrase:

Is **Fred** ***planning*** **his vacation already?** The verb phrase is *is planning.*

Have **they** ***been working*** **late again?** The verb phrase is *have been working.*

As you may have already noticed, all the forms of *be* commonly are used as helpers: *be, am, is, are, was, were, been,* and *being.* In addition, the following also are used often:

has, have, had	**do, does, did**
can, could, may, might	**shall, will, should, would**

Checkup 4. Underline the verb phrase. Then circle the main verb.

1. She should have answered the ad sooner.
2. You may leave at noon.
3. Will you be there on time?
4. They have been writing to us for approval.
5. Only Bill had submitted his report on schedule.

Participles in Verb Phrases. Most of the main verbs in verb phrases are called *participles.* Participles are verb forms that can team up with helping verbs. There are two kinds of participles, present and past. Present participles always end in *ing.*

am revis*ing*	**has been cook*ing***
will be revis*ing*	**is cook*ing***

Revising and *cooking* are present participles of the basic verbs *revise* and *cook.* (Note that you must drop a final *e* before you add *ing* to *revise.*)

Past participles also are easy to form. For all regular verbs, you simply add *d* or *ed* to form the past participle.

have revise*d*	**has been cook*ed***
had revise*d*	**will be cook*ed***

Revised and *cooked* are past participles of the basic verbs *revise* and *cook*. If a verb ends in *e*, add *d* to form its past participle. If it does not end in *e*, add *ed* to form its past participle.

Notice the word *part* in *participle*; use it to remember that a participle is only *part* of the complete verb phrase—it needs a helper.

Basic Verbs in Verb Phrases. We have just seen how *revising, cooking, revised,* and *cooked* can be used in verb phrases. As you will see later, the basic verbs *revise* and *cook* also may be used in verb phrases:

will revise **will cook**

To sum up, then, the main verb in a verb phrase may be a participle (such as *revising, cooking, revised, cooked*) or a basic verb (*revise, cook*).

Checkup 5. In the appropriate blank, write the correct present and past participles for each verb given. Watch your spelling!

1. *ask:*	she is ____________	we have ____________
2. *paint:*	I am ____________	they had ____________
3. *attend:*	we are ____________	Miss Halsby has ____________

VERB TENSE

Tense simply means the time shown by a verb. Let's look at a few basics that will help you choose the right verb to express the exact tense—or time—you want.

Present Tense. The present form of the verb can show three different kinds of present action or condition.

1. A present action: **I *need* help. Paul *wants* the job.**
2. A continual or habitual action: **The clerk *orders* supplies on Friday. He *awakens* early.**
3. A timeless truth: **Love *conquers* all.**

Most of the time, you use the present tense to show that something is happening *now*. In your everyday speech, you use present tense forms with the pronouns *I, you, he, she, it, we,* and *they* very frequently:

I work	**we work**
you work	**you work**
he / she / it } works	**they work**

You've probably noticed that *work* is used with all the pronouns except *he, she,* and *it*. In the present tense, the verb form used with *he, she,* or *it* must always end in *s;* for example, *he works, she works, it works.*

Look at this example:

I type	**we type**
you type	**you type**
he / she / it } types	**they type**

Now notice that the following example adds an *es* when it is used with *he, she,* or *it*:

I watch	**we watch**
you watch	**you watch**
he / she / it } watches	**they watch**

As you see, you add *s* to *type* to get *he types, she types, it types.* For *watch,* however, and for all other verbs that end in *ch, sh, s, x,* or *z,* you must add *es.* For example, *he pushes, she passes, it washes.* (You've probably already noticed the similarity with the plurals of nouns ending in *ch, sh, s, x,* and *z.* To form their plurals, they, too, add *es.*)

Thus you see the following general pattern for present tense verbs:

I ________________	**we** ________________
you ________________	**you** ________________
he / she / it } ________________**s (*or* es)**	**they** ________________

You may fill in the blanks with any basic verb: *talk, place, ask, want, provide, interview, dance,* and many others. Just be sure that you add *s* (or *es*) with *he, she,* and *it.*

You have seen that an *s* (or *es*) is added to the present tense verb used with *he, she,* or *it*: *he types, she lives, it works,* and so on. The same verb form is used with singular nouns: *Kenneth types, Mary lives, the machine works.* The reason is obvious. *He* is a pronoun substitute for *Kenneth* (both are singular). *She* is a pronoun substitute for *Mary* (both are singular). *It* is a pronoun substitute for *the machine* (both are singular).

Plural nouns use the same present tense form as the plural pronoun *they*:

they type	**they live**	**they work**
the men type	**the women live**	**the machines work**

Obviously, *they* can serve as a substitute for *the men,* for *the women,* or for *the machines.* All, therefore, use the same present tense form.

Checkup 6. Fill in the blanks with the correct present tense verb for each pronoun and noun.

1. *work:* I ________ you ________ it ________
2. *push:* we ________ it ________ the truck ________
3. *crash:* the car ________ he ________ planes ________
4. *talk:* we ________ managers ________ they ________
5. *prepare:* she ________ he ________ executives ________

Past Tense. The past form of a verb tells about something that has already happened. The past tense form of a verb stands alone; it has no helper.

We *lived* in San Diego last year. **We *ordered* a new desk.**
Lived and *ordered* are past tense verbs.

For all regular verbs, the past tense is formed very easily—in fact, it is formed exactly as the past participle is formed. You add *d* to basic verbs that end in *e*, and you add *ed* to basic verbs that do not end in *e*. For example, let's form the past tense of the verbs *skate* and *call*:

I skate*d* **we skate*d***
you skate*d* **you skate*d***
he / she / it } skate*d* **they skate*d***

I call*ed* **we call*ed***
you call*ed* **you call*ed***
he / she / it } call*ed* **they call*ed***

Notice that there is only one form used with *all* pronouns and *all* nouns. There are no variations.

Perhaps you're wondering, "What is the difference between the past tense *called* and the past participle *called*?" The difference lies only in their use. A past tense *never* has a helper; a past participle *always* has a helper because it's part of a verb phrase.

I *called* him. Because *called* has no helper, it must be a past tense.
I have *called* him. Because *called* has a helper, *have called* is a past participle.

Checkup 7. Fill in the blanks with the correct past tense verb for each pronoun and noun.

1. *complete:* he ________ we ________ Brett ________
2. *scatter:* she ________ it ________ machines ________
3. *remove:* they ________ you ________ the polish ________

Future Tense. The future tense forms also are simple to form because there are no variations. The same form is used with all pronouns and all nouns:

I will arrive	**we will arrive**
you will arrive	**you will arrive**
he / she / it } will arrive	**they will arrive**

I will stop	**we will stop**
you will stop	**you will stop**
he / she / it } will stop	**they will stop**

The future tense *will arrive* and *will stop* also are used with all nouns, singular and plural.

The man *will arrive.*	**The members *will arrive.***
The machine *will stop.*	**The cars *will stop.***

Because there are no variations, the future tense is easy to use.

Checkup 8. Fill in the blanks with the correct future tense verb for each pronoun and noun.

1. *go:* I ______ Brenda ______
2. *prepare:* we ______ the assistants ______
3. *approve:* they ______ Ms. Williams ______
4. *recommend:* she ______ Mrs. Hatter ______
5. *revise:* you ______ our supervisor ______

The three tenses we've just studied—the present, the past, and the future—do *not* require participles. Now let's move on to the tenses that do require participles. Let's begin with the perfect tenses. They are called *perfect* because they show action that has been completed, or "perfected."

Present Perfect Tense. The present perfect tense shows an action that was completed in the past or an action that was begun in the past and continues into the present. The present perfect tense is formed by using the helper *have* or *has* plus a past participle (*H* = helper; *PP* = past participle).

H + PP
↓ ↓

Bertha and Daniel *have received* graduate degrees. *Have received* shows action completed in the past.

She *has received* only 14 responses so far. *Has received* shows action that began in the past and continues into the present, because she is *still* receiving responses.

You use the helper *has* with *he, she, it,* and any singular noun.

he *has* received — **it *has* stopped**
she *has* ordered — **the bus *has* arrived**

You use the helper *have* with *I, you, we, they,* and any plural noun.

I *have* delivered — **we *have* interviewed**
you *have* accepted — **they *have* shipped**

Checkup 9. Fill in the blanks with the correct present perfect tense verb for each pronoun and verb.

1. *produce:* we ____________ Mark ____________
2. *audit:* she ____________ Mrs. Ames ____________
3. *delay:* Wes ____________ they ____________
4. *submit:* I ____________ you ____________
5. *prepare:* Anna ____________ my assistant ____________

Past Perfect Tense. Whenever you have two actions, both of which happened in the past, use the past perfect tense to show which of the two actions occurred first. For example:

H ↓ PP ↓

The plane *had left* by the time we arrived.

This sentence uses two verbs to describe two past actions: (1) *had left* and (2) *arrived.* Let's assume that we arrived at 2:15 p.m. and that the plane had left at 2 p.m. The verb *had left* makes it clear that this is the action that happened *first.* The past tense *arrived* shows that this is the action that happened *second.*

The past perfect tense is always formed by joining the helper *had* with a past participle. Here are other examples in which the past perfect tense and the past tense are used together to distinguish clearly between *two* past actions.

They *had filled* the position before I applied. First they filled the position; then I applied.

Sheila sent me a copy, but her assistant *had sent* me one already. First the assistant sent a copy; then Sheila sent one.

Checkup 10. Fill in the blanks with the correct past perfect tense verb for each pronoun and noun.

1. *type:* I ____________ Mr. Sloane ____________
2. *develop:* we ____________ she ____________
3. *call:* Barry ____________ Mrs. Unseld ____________
4. *plan:* you ____________ all of us ____________
5. *analyze:* she ____________ the managers ____________

Future Perfect Tense. A future perfect tense verb is used to show that an action will be completed or perfected at some definite time in the future. The future perfect tense is formed by using the helper *will have* plus a past participle.

H PP

By next Friday I *will have bought* the tickets. *Will have bought* shows that this action will be completed at a specific future time—*by next Friday.*

Before May 1 they *will have filled* the position. The position isn't filled yet, but it will be filled *before May 1.*

In 1989 our company *will have been* in business for 100 years. As of today, the company has *not* been in business for 100 years; however, by a specific future time—*in 1989*—the company *will have been* in business for 100 years.

The future perfect tense is formed by joining the helper *will have* with a past participle.

Checkup 11. Fill in the blanks with the correct future perfect tense verb for each pronoun and noun.

1. *paint:* they ______________ my wife and I ______________
2. *approve:* she ______________ we ______________
3. *hire:* I ______________ our department ______________
4. *use:* we ______________ you ______________

As you can see, then, the perfect tenses use a form of *have* plus a past participle:

	H	+ PP
Present Perfect:	***has* or *have***	**+ past participle**
Past Perfect:	***had***	**+ past participle**
Future Perfect:	***will have***	**+ past participle**

The present perfect uses the present tense of *have* (*have* and *has*), the past perfect uses the past tense of *have* (*had*), and the future perfect uses the future tense of *have* (*will have*)—all with a past participle, of course!

Now let's see how present participles are used in verb phrases. Present participles are used as main verbs (the last verb in a verb phrase) in the progressive tenses, tenses that show action in progress.

Present Progressive Tense. The present progressive tense is formed by joining the present tense helper *am, is,* or *are* with a present participle.

I *am driving* to Detroit, and Shirley *is flying* to St. Paul. Both of us *are leaving* on the same day, Saturday. *Am driving, is flying,* and *are leaving* are all present progressive tenses.

Past Progressive Tense. The past progressive tense is formed by joining the past tense helper *was* or *were* with a present participle.

Jane *was ordering* dinner while we *were paying* our bill. *Was ordering* and *were paying* are past progressive tenses.

Future Progressive Tense. The future progressive tense is formed by joining the future tense helper *will be* with a present participle.

The company *will be giving* bonuses at the end of this year.

For the first time, all employees *will be receiving* bonuses. *Will be giving* and *will be receiving* are future progressive tense verbs.

As you see, then, the progressive tenses are formed as follows:

	H	+	PP
Present Progressive:	*am, is* **or** *are*	+	**present participle**
Past Progressive:	*was* **or** *were*	+	**present participle**
Future Progressive:	*will be*	+	**present participle**

Checkup 12. Fill in the blanks with the correct progressive tense verb for each pronoun and noun.

	PRESENT PROGRESSIVE	PAST PROGRESSIVE	FUTURE PROGRESSIVE
1. *gain:*	I ________	you ________	Jack ________
2. *hold:*	she ________	they ________	you ________
3. *pull:*	he ________	Bill ________	it ________

Perfect Progressive Tenses. As you speak and write, you sometimes need to form verb phrases such as the following:

Our company *has been losing* money for two years.

Our company *had been losing* money when I joined the firm.

By the end of this year, our company *will have been losing* money for three consecutive years.

These verb phrases look complicated, but they are easy to form:

	H	+	PP
Present Perfect Progressive:	*has been* **or** *have been*	+	**present participle**
Past Perfect Progressive:	*had been*	+	**present participle**
Future Perfect Progressive:	*will have been*	+	**present participle**

Notice that (1) *has been* or *have been* is the present tense helper, (2) *had been* is the past tense helper, and (3) *will have been* is the future tense helper. In addition, notice that (4) all use *been* plus a present participle.

To prepare for a quiz on verbs, review all the sections in this lesson. Make sure that you can form *all* the verb tenses correctly.

REVIEW QUIZ

On a separate sheet of paper, write a sentence using the following verbs.

1. was checking
2. has cleaned
3. have delivered
4. had inspected
5. will share
6. will have completed
7. wrote
8. has spoken
9. have been losing

Irregular and Problem Verbs

In Lesson 8, you probably noticed that all verb forms are derived from four principal parts: the present tense and the past tense, and the present participle and the past participle. You saw that there is a pattern for forming these principal parts:

PRESENT TENSE	PAST TENSE	PRESENT PARTICIPLE	PAST PARTICIPLE
type/types	**typed**	**typing**	**typed**
walk/walks	**walked**	**walking**	**walked**

As you remember, the present tense form (we called it the basic verb) adds an *s* when it is used with *he, she, it,* or a singular noun. Thus there are two present tense forms for each verb. The past tense is formed by adding *d* or *ed.*

The participles are also easy to form. For the present participle, we add *ing* to the basic verb, and the past participle is formed exactly the same as the past tense. These verbs are called *regular* when their forms follow this pattern. They are called *irregular* when they do not.

Checkup 1. Fill in the blanks with the correct verb forms.

	PRESENT TENSE	PAST TENSE	PRESENT PARTICIPLE	PAST PARTICIPLE
1.	*arrive/arrives*	__________	__________	__________
2.	*wave/waves*	__________	__________	__________
3.	*delay/delays*	__________	__________	__________

IRREGULAR VERBS

There is no such pattern for irregular verbs, as the following list shows:

PRESENT TENSE	PAST TENSE	PRESENT PARTICIPLE	PAST PARTICIPLE
be (am, is, are)	**was, were**	**being**	**been**
become	**became**	**becoming**	**become**
come	**came**	**coming**	**come**
do	**did**	**doing**	**done**

PRESENT TENSE	PAST TENSE	PRESENT PARTICIPLE	PAST PARTICIPLE
flee	**fled**	**fleeing**	**fled**
get	**got**	**getting**	**has got** *or* **gotten**
go	**went**	**going**	**gone**
have	**had**	**having**	**had**
hold	**held**	**holding**	**held**
lead	**led**	**leading**	**led**
make	**made**	**making**	**made**
meet	**met**	**meeting**	**met**
say	**said**	**saying**	**said**
stand	**stood**	**standing**	**stood**
strike	**struck**	**striking**	**struck**
win	**won**	**winning**	**won**

Although there is no one pattern for irregular verbs, there are similarities among many of them. Read the following list carefully—better yet, use each word in a sentence. (Remember that the participles will need helpers!) As you read them, note the similarities of the sounds of many of the verb forms (*keep, sleep,* and *weep,* for example). Note, too, that with few exceptions the past tense and the past participle do not end in *d,* as they do for *all* regular verbs. Study these verbs carefully.

	PRESENT TENSE	PAST TENSE	PRESENT PARTICIPLE	PAST PARTICIPLE
a.	**arise**	**arose**	**arising**	**arisen**
	fall	**fell**	**falling**	**fallen**
	forbid	**forbade**	**forbidding**	**forbidden**
	give	**gave**	**giving**	**given**
	hide	**hid**	**hiding**	**hidden**
	mistake	**mistook**	**mistaking**	**mistaken**
	shake	**shook**	**shaking**	**shaken**
	strive	**strove**	**striving**	**striven**
	take	**took**	**taking**	**taken**
	typewrite	**typewrote**	**typewriting**	**typewritten**
	underwrite	**underwrote**	**underwriting**	**underwritten**

	PRESENT TENSE	PAST TENSE	PRESENT PARTICIPLE	PAST PARTICIPLE
b.	**blow**	**blew**	**blowing**	**blown**
	draw	**drew**	**drawing**	**drawn**
	fly	**flew**	**flying**	**flown**
	grow	**grew**	**growing**	**grown**
	know	**knew**	**knowing**	**known**
	swear	**swore**	**swearing**	**sworn**
	tear	**tore**	**tearing**	**torn**
	withdraw	**withdrew**	**withdrawing**	**withdrawn**

	PRESENT TENSE	PAST TENSE	PRESENT PARTICIPLE	PAST PARTICIPLE
c.	bend	bent	bending	bent
	deal	dealt	dealing	dealt
	feel	felt	feeling	felt
	keep	kept	keeping	kept
	lend	lent	lending	lent
	sleep	slept	sleeping	slept
	spend	spent	spending	spent
	weep	wept	weeping	wept

	PRESENT TENSE	PAST TENSE	PRESENT PARTICIPLE	PAST PARTICIPLE
d.	begin	began	beginning	begun
	drink	drank	drinking	drunk
	ring	rang	ringing	rung
	run	ran	running	run
	shrink	shrank	shrinking	shrunk
	sing	sang	singing	sung
	swim	swam	swimming	swum

	PRESENT TENSE	PAST TENSE	PRESENT PARTICIPLE	PAST PARTICIPLE
e.	break	broke	breaking	broken
	choose	chose	choosing	chosen
	forget	forgot	forgetting	forgotten
	steal	stole	stealing	stolen

	PRESENT TENSE	PAST TENSE	PRESENT PARTICIPLE	PAST PARTICIPLE
f.	buy	bought	buying	bought
	seek	sought	seeking	sought
	teach	taught	teaching	taught

Of all the irregular verbs, the ones most commonly used are *be, do,* and *have.* Let's look at these closely.

To Be. *To be* is the oddest of all the irregulars, and it is also one of the most commonly used verbs. You use it hundreds of times each week as you speak and write. Note the forms of *to be*:

Present Tense:	**I am**	**we are**
	you are	**you are**
	he / she / it } is	**they are**

This is the only verb that has *three* forms—*am, is,* and *are*—in its present tense. (All the others have two: *type/types, begin/begins,* and so on.)

Past Tense:	I was	we were
	you were	you were
	he, she, it } was	they were

It also is the only verb that has *two* forms—*was* and *were*—in its past tense. (All the others have one.)

Future Tense:	I will be	we will be
	you will be	you will be
	he, she, it } will be	they will be

To Do. Let's look at the forms of *to do*:

Present Tense:	I do	we do
	you do	you do
	he, she, it } does	they do

Past Tense:	I did	we did
	you did	you did
	he, she, it } did	they did

Future Tense:	I will do	we will do
	you will do	you will do
	he, she, it } will do	they will do

Like all other verbs, the present tense has two forms: *do* and *does*. Note that *does* is used only with *he, she, it,* or a singular noun.

To Have. Here are the forms of *to have*:

Present Tense:	I have	we have
	you have	you have
	he, she, it } has	they have

Past Tense:	I had	we had
	you had	you had
	he, she, it } had	they had

Future Tense:	**I will have**	**we will have**
	you will have	**you will have**
	he / she / it will have	**they will have**

Again, note that in the present tense *has* is the form that is used with *he, she, it,* or a singular noun.

Similarities. Although the irregular verbs follow no one pattern, there are "laws" that govern the use of *all* verbs, regular and irregular:

1. For *all* verbs, the present tense form used with *he, she, it,* or a singular noun ends in *s*.

he is	**the car runs**
she does	**Tom buys**
it has	**my boss knows**

2. A past tense *never* has a helper, whether the verb is regular or irregular.

we paid	**he typed**
she ordered	**the men arrived**
Bill spoke	**Ms. Halston bought**

3. A participle *always* has a helper, whether the verb is regular or irregular.

we *have* paid	**he *has* typed**
she *has* ordered	**the men *have* arrived**
Bill *has* spoken	**Ms. Halston *has* bought**

Checkup 2. On a separate sheet of paper, label four columns "Present Tense," "Past Tense," "Present Participle," and "Past Participle." Under each column, write the appropriate form of the following verbs. (***Note:*** Your teacher may also ask you to write sentences for some or all of these principal parts.)

1. be	6. feel	11. begin
2. do	7. run	12. write
3. have	8. buy	13. give
4. take	9. fall	14. make
5. know	10. speak	15. fly

Now correct any verb errors in the following sentences. Underline the error and write your correction in the space provided.

16. He has did all the work that we assigned to him. 16. ________________
17. We been busy all morning. 17. ________________
18. Vera has spoke to Miss Trent about the book. 18. ________________
19. She do very good work. 19. ________________
20. Production has fell in the last two months. 20. ________________

PROBLEM VERBS

A few verbs that you use every day cause more than their share of trouble. Here are some common troublemakers:

Lie/Lay. *Lie* means "to rest" or "to recline." This verb has no object.

The doctor advised the patient to *lie* still.
Infants often *lie* and sleep for hours.

There is no object that receives the action of the verb *lie*.

Lay means "to place" or "to put something." This verb *always* has an object that receives the action. Something is placed or put.

We have to *lay* the foundation first. The *foundation* receives the action of being laid. *Foundation* is the object of the verb *lay.* Lay what? *Foundation.*

***Lay* the carbons on top of the file.** The *carbons* receive the action of being laid. *Carbons* is the object of the verb *lay.* Lay what? *Carbons.*

The principal parts of *to lie* are *lie*, *lay*, *lying*, and *lain*. The principal parts of *to lay* are *lay*, *laid*, *laying*, and *laid*. Let's see how these forms are used. Study the following examples.

Present: *lie, lies*
I *lie* down to rest daily.
He *lies* down to rest daily.

Past: *lay*
I *lay* down to rest yesterday.
She *lay* down to rest yesterday.

Present Participle: *lying*
I was *lying* down.
He was *lying* down.

Past Participle: *lain*
I have *lain* down to rest each day.
He has *lain* down to rest each day.

Present: *lay, lays*
I always *lay* the letter on his desk.
She *lays* the letters on his desk each morning.

Past: *laid*
I *laid* the letters on his desk.
He *laid* the letters on his desk.

Present Participle: *laying*
I was *laying* the letters on his desk.
He was *laying* the letters on his desk.

Past Participle: *laid*
I have *laid* the letters there daily.
They have *laid* the letters there also.

Notice that the verbs *lay*, *laid*, *laying*, and *laid* always have objects (in the examples above the object is *letters*) that receive the action.

Clue: If you're not sure whether you need *lay* (which always has an object) or *lie* (which never has an object), use this little trick. Substitute either *place* or *put* for the verb. If the sentence still makes sense, use a form of *lay*, because *lay* means to place something or to put something. On the other hand, if *place* or *put* doesn't make sense, use a form of *lie.*

Will you *lay* the books on the table? You can substitute *put the books* and the sentence still makes sense. *Lay* has an object. Lay what? *Books.*

I *laid* the transcript on his desk. You can substitute *put the transcript. Laid* has an object. Laid what? *Transcript.*

Please *lay* still so the doctor can examine you. You can't substitute *put* or *place*. *Lay* has no object. Lay what? No answer, because nothing receives the action.

Corrected: **Please *lie* still so the doctor can examine you.**

She *laid* down to rest an hour ago. Since you can't logically substitute *put*, you need to use a form of the verb *lie*—in this case, the past tense *lay*. *Laid* has no object. Laid what? No answer.

Corrected: **She *lay* down to rest an hour ago.**

Notice that the present tense of *to lay* and the past tense of *to lie* (*lay*) are identical. That's one of the reasons these verbs cause trouble. *Lay*, the past tense of *lie*, just doesn't "sound like" a past tense verb to most of us. It has a "soft" sound. Because you are used to adding a *d* to form the past tense, you might be tempted to say "I *laid* down for a few minutes after dinner," instead of "I *lay* down for a few minutes after dinner." But remember—*laid* has to have an object, a receiver of the action. *Lay* as a past tense of *lie* has no object.

You may say: **I *laid* the package down ten minutes ago.**
You must not say: **I *laid* down ten minutes ago.**
You may say: **I *lay* down ten minutes ago.**

Laid can mean only one thing—something was placed or put somewhere. Never use *laid* as the past tense of *to lie*.

Remember, too, that these verbs, like all verbs, use a helper with the participle but not with the past tense. Remember the clue: A participle is only *part* of a verb phrase; it needs a helper to be complete.

Checkup 3. Fill in the correct form of *lie* or *lay*. Then underline the object of each.

1. I went home to ______________ down.
2. I had ______________ the money on the table before I went to bed.
3. Just ______________ the magazine on the end table.
4. She must have ______________ in the sun too long.
5. I fell asleep the minute I ______________ down.
6. We have ______________ our plans carefully.

Sit/Set. *Sit* means "to be seated" or "to occupy a position." This verb does not have a receiver of the action.

How can they *sit* on those uncomfortable benches? Sit what? No answer, because there is no receiver of the action.

The work will just *sit* there until tomorrow. Sit what? No answer.

There are no objects receiving the action of *sit*.

Set means "to put" or "to place something." This verb always has a receiver of the action.

Judy *set* the dictaphone on the desk. Set what? *Dictaphone*.
The movers *set* the chairs in neat rows. Set what? *Chairs*.

The principal parts of *to sit* are *sit*, *sat*, *sitting*, and *sat*. The principal parts of *to set* are *set*, *set*, *setting*, and *set*.

***Present:* sit, sits**
I usually *sit* in the balcony.
She usually *sits* in the balcony.

***Past:* sat**
I *sat* in the balcony.
She *sat* in the balcony.

***Present Participle:* sitting**
I was *sitting* in the balcony.

They were *sitting* in the balcony.

***Past Participle:* sat**
I have *sat* in the balcony.
She has *sat* in the balcony.

***Present:* set, sets**
I usually *set* the alarm for 7 a.m.
She *sets* her alarm for 7:30.

***Past:* set**
Yesterday I *set* the alarm earlier.
Yesterday she *set* the alarm earlier.

***Present Participle:* setting**
I am *setting* the alarm earlier for tomorrow.
She is *setting* the alarm earlier for tomorrow.

***Past Participle:* set**
I have *set* the alarm already.
She has *set* the alarm already.

Notice that *set* works just like *lay*. Both *set* and *lay* have objects—something is set or is laid somewhere. Again, if you can substitute *put* or *place* for *set*, then *set* is correct. If not, use a form of *sit*.

Checkup 4. Fill in the correct form of *sit* or *set*. Then underline the objects of the verb *set*.

1. Please ______________ the coffee pot over there.
2. When we're through, we will ______________ here for lunch.
3. I have ______________ the papers aside for awhile.
4. Have you ever ______________ by the window at noon?
5. We ______________ and watched while the workers ______________ up the display.
6. While we were ______________ in the conference room, Mr. Colombo ______________ up the audiovisual equipment.

Rise/Raise. *Rise* means "to get up," "to arise," or "to ascend." This verb does *not* have a receiver of the action. Just like the no-object verbs *lie* and *sit*, *rise* has no object.

Raise means "to lift" or "to make something higher." It also means "to grow" or "to cultivate." This verb *always* has an object that receives the action—something is raised.

The chairperson *rose* to bring the committee meeting to order.
He *rises* promptly each morning at 6 a.m.
The owner *raised* everyone's salary.
John *raises* exotic tropical plants as a hobby.

The principal parts of *rise* are *rise, rose, rising,* and *risen.* The principal parts of *raise* are *raise, raised, raising,* and *raised.*

Present: rise/rises
I always *rise* early.
She always *rises* early.

Past: rose
The balloon *rose* slowly

Present Participle: rising
Inflation is *rising* at a rate of 15 percent annually.

Past Participle: risen
Prices have *risen.*

Present: raise/raises
Please *raise* the window.
She *raises* thoroughbred horses.

Past: raised
They *raised* the flag.

Present Participle: raising
They are *raising* the flag now.

Past Participle: raised
He has *raised* prices.

Checkup 5. Fill in the correct form of *rise* or *raise.* Then underline the objects of the verb *raise.*

1. His favorite cliche is "We must ____________ to the occasion."
2. Please ____________ your hand when you bid.
3. Have we ____________ our productivity this month?
4. Expenses have ____________ every month.
5. They ____________ and applauded the speaker.
6. The new manager ____________ our salaries.

Affect/Effect. *Affect* is a verb meaning "to influence," "to produce a change in," or "to make an impression on." This verb always has an object—a thing or person that is influenced, changed, or impressed.

How did the strike *affect* (*influence* or *change*) our profits? Affect what? *Profits.*
Our plea did not *affect* (*influence* or *change*) the committee's decision. Affect what? *Decision*.

Effect is a verb meaning "to bring about." It has limited use as a verb. When *effect* is used, it always has an object. To test whether you should use *effect* as your verb, try substituting the words *bring about.*

We cannot *effect (bring about)* the changes you want. Effect what? *Changes.*
Those negotiations will *effect* (*bring about*) peace. Effect what? *Peace.*

Effect is most commonly used as a noun meaning "the result or impression caused by some action." Think of *aftereffect* to help you remember that the noun *effect* means "the result."

The reorganization had no *effect* (*result*) on me.
The *effect* (*result*) was more than we expected.

Checkup 6. Fill in the correct form of *affect* or *effect*.

1. The ______________ of the announcement was anger.
2. His speech did not ______________ me at all.
3. The policy changes were intended to ______________ harmony.
4. Will this news ______________ your decision?
5. What did you hope would be the ______________ of this policy change?

Were. As you have seen, the verbs *was* and *were* are past tense forms of *to be*:

I was	**we were**
you were	**you were**
he / she / it } was	**they were**

Was is used with *I, he, she,* and *it,* as well as with singular nouns. However, there are two exceptions to this usage.

1. Following *if, as if,* and *as though*, the verb *was* is replaced by *were*. *If, as if,* and *as though* generally describe situations that are not true or that are highly unlikely; in such situations, *were* is the correct verb.

   If I *were* younger, I'd join the race. But I'm not younger; therefore, you say "if I *were*," not "if I *was*."

   He acts as if he *were* the president of the company. But he's not the president of the company; therefore, you say "as if he *were*," not "as if he *was*."

   She spends money as though she *were* wealthy. But you know that she's not wealthy; therefore, you say "as though she *were*," not "as though she *was*."

2. Following the verb *wish*, the verb *was* is also replaced by *were* because again we have an "if" situation—something that isn't true at the present time.

   I wish I *were* the manager of the department. But I'm not the manager; therefore, you say "wish I *were*," not "wish I *was*."

   We all wish that he *were* happier in his job. But he isn't; therefore, you say "wish he *were*," not "wish he *was*."

Checkup 7. Fill in the blanks with *was* or *were*, whichever is correct.

1. I wish I ______________ going with you.
2. Jack said he wishes he ______________ able to come with us, but he will be out of town.
3. I noticed that Anthony often acts as though he ______________ the owner of this company.

4. Mr. Hanes retired two years ago, but it seems as if it ______________ yesterday.

5. If Ms. Carlton ______________ still our manager, we would have fewer problems.

6. Mrs. Beau ______________ here earlier this morning.

7. Our manager ______________ satisfied with their results.

REVIEW QUIZ

Part 1. Underline the correct verb in the following sentences.

1. When the bell had (rang, rung) twice, we (raised, rose) from our seats.
2. Because our costs have (raised, risen) each year, we have had to (raise, rise) our selling prices.
3. (Sit, Set) here—or better yet, (lie, lay) down on the couch.
4. Janice has (did, done) an expert job; she has (wrote, written) effective advertisements for the new product.
5. He acts as if I (was, were) the person who had (broke, broken) that priceless antique!

Part 2. Correct any verb errors in the following sentences. Underline the error and write your correction in the space provided. Write C if a sentence is correct.

1. Francine has did all her work for next week's marketing conference. 1. ______________
2. Mrs. DeMott been with our company for almost ten years. 2. ______________
3. Everyone agrees that she should have spoke to her supervisor about the problem. 3. ______________
4. If you don't feel well, perhaps you should lie down for a few minutes. 4. ______________
5. All the marketing representatives said that Carol done a good job of coordinating the meeting. 5. ______________
6. Because we had flew for nearly ten hours, we were exhausted when we reached Buenos Aires. 6. ______________
7. For the third consecutive year, our sales goals been risen more than 20 percent. 7. ______________
8. Have they chosen a site for the branch office? 8. ______________
9. Her business has grew dramatically since 1976. 9. ______________
10. I think that Mrs. Fredericks had already went. 10. ______________

SECTION 3 WRAP-UP:
Verbs

The next several pages of reminders and spelling rules will help you wrap up what you need to know about verbs. Be sure to check back in this section if you have any questions.

REMINDERS

The following statements are reminders of common, irritating mistakes in the use of verbs that are found in everyday business correspondence. We've already talked about them. Do your best to avoid these mistakes.

Error: **He *don't* mind working late.**

A third person singular subject (*he, she, it*) requires the verb *does* (not *do*) and *doesn't* (not *don't*). Review these forms of the verb *do*:

I
you } **do** *or* **don't**
we
they

he
she } **does** *or* **doesn't**
it

Correction: **He *doesn't* mind working late.**

Error: **They *done* the job well.** **I *been* promoted.**

Done and *been* are participles. They can't stand alone! They need a helping verb (for example, *have, has,* or *had*) to complete the verb phrase. Past tenses, on the other hand, do stand alone. Whether you use the past tense alone or the participle with a helper depends on the time of the action you want to describe. Either can be correct, depending on your meaning. But never use the participle alone!

Correction (past tense): **They *did* the job well.** **I *was* promoted.**
Correction (past perfect tense): **They *have done* the job well.**
I *have been* promoted.

Error: **I *laid* down to take a nap.**

The past tense of *lie* is *lay*! *Laid* means "to put" or "to place something." Since *placed* or *put* cannot be substituted, *laid* is not correct in this sentence.

Correction: **I *lay* down to take a nap.**

Error: ***Lay* down if you don't feel well.**

Here, the present tense *lie* is needed. *Place* or *put* cannot be substituted.

Correction: ***Lie* down if you don't feel well.**

Error: **We were *setting* there discussing the convention.**

Setting always has an object—a receiver of the action. What were you setting? No answer. Since you cannot substitute *placing*, *setting* is not the correct verb in this sentence.

Correction: **We were *sitting* there discussing the convention.**

SPELLING OF VERBS

To get maximum power from verbs, you have to be sure that they're correctly spelled. Misspelled words draw your reader's attention away from your intended message. You want your readers to concentrate on what you're saying, not on how your words look.

Many misspellings happen when verbs are changed into past or present participles by adding *ed* or *ing*. Not all verbs are changed in the same way. Notice these differences.

One-Syllable Verbs Ending in a Single Vowel Plus a Single Consonant. Before adding *ed* or *ing* to form the past tense or past participle of these words, double the final consonant.

	VOWEL / CONSONANT	VOWEL / CONSONANT
Present:	**flap**	**ban**
Past Tense and Past Participle (double consonant, then add **ed***):*	**flapped**	**banned**
Present Participle (double consonant, then add **ing***):*	**flapping**	**banning**

Notice that doubling the final consonant gives these words a backbone of two consonants in the middle with one vowel on each side. For example, *banned* has a double-*n* backbone with a single *a* on one side and a single *e* on the other side, while *flapping* has a double-*p* backbone with a single *a* on one side and a single *i* on the other. This little trick will help you remember what to do with short, one-syllable verbs that have a single vowel before the final single consonant. Add *ed* or *ing*, but first give the verb a double-consonant backbone.

Checkup 1. Provide past tense, past participle, and present participle forms for the following verbs.

	ship	stop
Present:	ship	stop
1. *Past Tense:*	__________	__________
2. *Past Participle:*	__________	__________
3. *Present Participle:*	__________	__________

Two-Syllable Verbs Ending in a Single Vowel Plus a Single Consonant. Some of these words need a doubled consonant when you add *ed* or *ing,* and some do not. To decide which words need a double-letter backbone, pronounce the word and listen for the stress (the accent or emphasis).

1. When the stress is on the *second* half of the word, you need a double-letter backbone to support the two weaker ends. For example, when you add *ed* and *ing* to verbs like *de·fer′* and *com·pel′*, you double the *r* and the *l.*

	VOWEL / CONSONANT	VOWEL / CONSONANT
Present:	**defer**	**compel**
Past Tense and Past Participle:	**deferred**	**compelled**
Present Participle:	**deferring**	**compelling**

Remember: When the second syllable of these two-syllable verbs is stressed, double the consonant (to provide the double-letter backbone) before you add *ed* or *ing.*

Checkup 2. Provide past tense, past participle, and present participle forms for the following verbs.

	rebel	confer
Present:	rebel	confer
1. *Past Tense:*	__________	__________
2. *Past Participle:*	__________	__________
3. *Present Participle:*	__________	__________

2. When the stress is on the *first* half of the word, the word is pronounced with a strong, accented beginning and a soft ending. So you just add *ed* or *ing* without any doubling, and the ending stays soft. Notice how the stress stays on the beginning of the verbs *co′·ver* and *of′·fer* when you add *ed* and *ing.*

	VOWEL / CONSONANT	VOWEL / CONSONANT
Present:	**cover**	**offer**
Past Tense and Past Participle:	**cover ed**	**offer ed**
Present Participle:	**cover ing**	**offer ing**

The final single consonant remains single, with a single vowel on each side. ***Remember:*** When the first syllable of these two-syllable verbs is stressed, just add *ed* or *ing* to the verb.

Checkup 3. Provide past tense, past participle, and present participle forms for the following verbs.

	suffer	season
Present:	suffer	season
1. *Past Tense:*	__________	__________
2. *Past Participle:*	__________	__________
3. *Present Participle:*	__________	__________

Verbs Ending in *E*. To form the past tense and past participle of verbs that already end in *e*, just add *d*:

	e ENDING	*e* ENDING
Present:	**reimburs*e***	**disagre*e***
Past Tense and Past Participle:	**reimburse*d***	**disagree*d***
	(ADD ONLY *d*)	(ADD ONLY *d*)

Checkup 4. Provide past tense and past participle forms for the following verbs.

1. retrieve __________ 2. free __________ 3. charge __________

To form the present participle of verbs ending in a silent *e* (that is, an *e* that is not pronounced), drop the *e* before adding *ing*:

	SILENT *e*	SILENT *e*
Present:	**reimburs*e***	**believ*e***
Present Participle:	**reimbursing**	**believing**
	(DROP *e*)	(DROP *e*)

If the final *e* is a pronounced *e*, do not drop the *e* when adding *ing*:

	SOUNDED *e*	SOUNDED *e*
Present:	**disagre*e***	**fre*e***
Present Participle:	**disagre*e* ing**	**fre*e* ing**
	(KEEP *e*)	(KEEP *e*)

Checkup 5. Give present participle forms for the following verbs.

1. retrieve __________ 3. be __________
2. see __________ 4. shape __________

Reminder: Notice these common exceptions to the rules covering *e*-ending verbs.

die/dying **dye/dyeing** **lie/lying** **tie/tying**

Verbs Ending in *Y*. The past tense and past participles of verbs that end in *y* may be formed in one of two ways.

1. When the final *y* has a consonant just before it, the *y* is changed to *i* before *ed* is added. The consonant before the *y* signals a change. (You used this same formula when you made plurals from *y*-ending nouns: *baby/babies*.)

	CONSONANT BEFORE *y*	CONSONANT BEFORE *y*
Present:	**scurry**	**marry**
Past Tense and Past Participle:	**scurried**	**married**
	(*y* TO *i*)	(*y* TO *i*)

2. But when the final *y* follows a vowel, *ed* is added without changing the *y*. (This, too, is the same rule you used in forming plurals of nouns ending in a vowel plus *y*: *turkey/turkeys*.)

	VOWEL BEFORE *y*	VOWEL BEFORE *y*
Present:	**play**	**decay**
Past Tense and Past Participle:	**played**	**decayed**
	(KEEP *y*)	(KEEP *y*)

Checkup 6. Provide past tense and past participle forms for the following verbs.

1. employ ______________
2. hurry ______________
3. delay ______________
4. fry ______________

To form the present participle of all *y*-ending verbs, just add *ing*:

scurry scurrying **decay decaying**

Checkup 7. Give present participle forms for the following verbs.

1. marry ______________ 2. play ______________ 3. fry ______________

Remember that your dictionary is your best reference for any unfamiliar spelling.

SPELLING EXERCISE

Use your dictionary to correct all misspelled verbs below. Write C after each verb that is correctly spelled. Then fill in the past tense, past participle, and present participle forms. Be ready for a spelling quiz on these words.

PRESENT	CORRECTION	PAST TENSE PAST PARTICIPLE	PRESENT PARTICIPLE
1. exajjerate	________	________	________
2. decieve	________	________	________

3. decend ______ ______ ______
4. embarass ______ ______ ______
5. aquaint ______ ______ ______
6. suceed ______ ______ ______
7. forfeit ______ ______ ______
8. aggrivate ______ ______ ______
9. intercede ______ ______ ______
10. inferr ______ ______ ______
11. procede ______ ______ ______
12. harrass ______ ______ ______
13. exseed ______ ______ ______
14. laber ______ ______ ______

Pronouns

YOUR GOALS

After finishing this section, you will be able to:

1. Choose correct personal pronouns according to whether a subject or an object is required.
2. Correctly form possessive pronouns.
3. Use pronouns that agree with the nouns they replace.
4. Avoid sex bias in the use of pronouns.
5. Recognize pronouns that are always singular, those that are always plural, and those that may be either singular or plural.
6. Correctly choose between *who* and *whom* and *whoever* and *whomever.*
7. Correctly spell and provide pronouns for 15 commonly misspelled words.

LESSON 11 Pronoun Forms and Uses

A pronoun, as you may recall, is a word that takes the place of a noun or nouns. By using a personal pronoun, you can avoid repeating the specific name of a person or thing. For example, how would you like to talk like this?

When Carl got into Carl's new car, Carl discovered that Carl had left the keys to Carl's new car on Carl's dresser.

Compare this shorter, less monotonous revision using pronouns:

When Carl got into *his* new car, *he* discovered that *he* had left the keys to *it* on *his* dresser.

You use pronouns in almost every message you put together, and most of the time you don't even think about it. But you need to know something about the kinds of pronouns and how they can be used. First let's look at a chart that shows pronoun forms and uses. The chart shows three kinds of pronouns—*subject, possessive,* and *objective* pronouns. The first person names the person speaking in a sentence. The second person names the person spoken to—the receiver of the action. The third person names the person or thing the message talks about.

FORMS OF THE PERSONAL PRONOUNS

	FIRST PERSON		SECOND PERSON		THIRD PERSON	
	SING.	PLURAL	SING.	PLURAL	SING.	PLURAL
Subject Form—These pronouns are used as a subject or as an identifying word after a being verb.	I	we	you	you	he she it	they
Possessive Form—These pronouns are used to show possession or ownership.	my mine	our ours	your yours	your yours	his her hers its	their theirs
Objective Forms—These pronouns are used as objects of verbs or prepositions.	me	us	you	you	him her it	them

SUBJECT FORMS

As Subjects of Verbs. Only naming pronouns can be used as subjects, even if you are using a double subject.

George and *she* are coming. ***Not:*** *George and her.*
Carrie and *I* will answer the phone. ***Not:*** *Carrie and me.*

You also need a subject form pronoun when the verb that goes with a pronoun subject is understood but not given.

He can afford it as well as *I*. Meaning "as well as *I* can afford it."
Not: as well as *me* can afford it.
We won as many awards as *they*. Meaning "as many awards as *they* won."
Not: as many awards as *them* won.

Checkup 1. Underline the correct pronouns.

1. When June and (me, I) left, the work was done.
2. I didn't get as much mail as (he, him).
3. Until (he, him) and (she, her) decide on a meeting place, we will not be able to meet with (they, them).

Following Being Verbs. Pronouns that follow a being verb simply identify, explain, or rename the subject. (The being verbs are *am, is, are, was, were, be, been,* and *being.*) In fact, being verbs act just like an arithmetic equals sign (=); that is, the figures or symbols on one side must equal the figures or symbols on the other side. So the subject and the identifying pronoun must be equal—both must be subject forms. The pronoun must be one that could be used as a subject.

The author of the book was *she*. ***Not:*** *her.*
The speaker they want is he. ***Not:*** *him.*

You can usually tell whether the pronoun is equal to the subject by trying to turn the sentence around. If the pronoun can be used as the subject, obviously a subject form pronoun is needed.

***She* was the *author* of the book.**
***He* is the *speaker* they want.**

Checkup 2. Underline the correct pronouns.

1. We didn't know that the owner was (he, him).
2. I think that my boss will be (she, her).
3. I answered the phone by saying, "This is (she, her)."

POSSESSIVE FORMS

Using Possessive Pronouns. Possessive pronouns act just like possessive nouns—they show possession, ownership, or origin. However, their forms are not alike. Possessive nouns are formed by using apostrophes. Possessive pronouns do *not* use apostrophes, even when they end in *s*.

his hers yours ours theirs its

Be very careful not to confuse these possessive pronouns with similar contractions that use apostrophes, especially in the case of *its* and *it's*. Look at the differences.

Possessive Pronoun:	**The policy has lost *its* effectiveness.**
Contraction:	**They say *it's* outdated.** *It is* outdated.
Possessive Pronoun:	***Your* policy is due for renewal.**
Contraction:	***You're* due to renew this policy.** *You are* due to . . . .
Possessive Pronoun:	***Their* terms are unreasonable.**
Contraction:	***They're* unreasonable.** *They are* unreasonable.
Possessive Pronoun:	**The company is *theirs*.**
Contraction:	***There's* another company to consider.** *There is* another . . . .

Checkup 3. Underline the correct pronouns.

1. We hope (your, you're) planning to come.
2. She claims that (its, it's) quality is superior.
3. Both of (their, they're) desks are battered.
4. (There's, Theirs) a new product on the market.
5. I don't think (its, it's) too late to order more.
6. If the fault is (theirs, there's), we'll soon know.

Before Verbal Nouns. Before verbal nouns (nouns formed from verbs, such as *running, cheating, typing*), a possessive pronoun is needed (not an objective pronoun).

I approve of *his* calling the client. *Not:* *him calling.*
Don't be surprised at *my* leaving early. *Not:* *me leaving.*

To understand why a possessive is needed, mentally put the words *act of* before the verbal noun, as follows:

I approve of *his* (act of) calling the client. If you used *him*, the sentence would suggest that the speaker approves of *him*, rather than approving of *his act of calling*.

Don't be surprised at *my* (act of) leaving early. If you used *me*, the sentence would suggest surprise over *me*, not over *my act of leaving early*.

Mark did not know about *their* (act of) changing the figures. If you used *them*, the suggestion would be that Mark did not know about *them*, rather than *their act of changing the figures*.

The words *act of* will help you to see that the pronoun needs to be possessive.

Checkup 4. Underline the correct pronouns.

1. Federal law prohibits (you, your) claiming such expenses as deductions.
2. We don't like (him, his) pressuring the customers.
3. Ms. Hann agreed to (me, my) transferring to another branch.

OBJECTIVE FORMS

Pronouns receiving the action of a verb or serving as objects of a preposition must be in the objective form. Check the chart again to review objective forms of pronouns. Then notice how these pronouns are used as objects of verbs and of prepositions.

Objects of Verbs. Objects of verbs—the persons or things that *receive* the action—must be in the objective form. Watch for double objects—two words that receive the action.

The supervisor selected *him* and *me* for the job. *Not: selected he and I.*
They asked *her* and *me* to write the article. *Not: asked she and I.*

Checkup 5. Underline the correct pronouns.

1. I hope they need (him, he) and (me, I) tomorrow.
2. If you want Karen and (me, I) to come early, let (us, we) know soon.
3. Their action hurts (them, they) more than it hurts (us, we).

Objects of Prepositions. Pronouns following prepositions must be in the objective case.

Three of *us* will write to *her*. *Us* is the object of the preposition *of*, and *her* is the object of *to*.

Here are some of the most commonly used prepositions:

in	**with**	**before**	**upon**
to	**above**	**beneath**	**under**
at	**beyond**	**below**	**except**
on	**besides**	**within**	**without**
of	**between**	**but**	

A few prepositions need special attention. The words *between, except,* and *but* (when *but* means *except*) are prepositions, but some speakers incorrectly use subject pronouns after them. Only objective pronouns must follow these and all other prepositions.

Let her sit between *you* and *me*. *Not:* *between you and I.*

Everyone agreed except *her*. *Not:* *except she.*

Everyone but *them* knew the plan. *Not:* *but they.*

Checkup 6. Underline the correct pronouns.

1. Between you and (I, me), I think it's too late.
2. Maybe we can get a new assignment for Red and (me, I).
3. Brenda and (I, me) will help you check these invoices.
4. Will they send copies to Mrs. Mann and (I, me)?
5. Send an acknowledgment to Mrs. Crest and (him, he).

PRONOUN PROBLEMS

Pronouns Joined to Other Pronouns or to Verbs. You've noticed that pronouns are often linked to nouns or to other pronouns; for example, *John and I, Betty and me; he or she, him and her.* How can you tell whether the subject form or the object form is correct? Easy. Just use each pronoun as if it were not linked to any noun or pronoun and your answer will become clear. Follow this simple two-step procedure:

1. Read the sentence.

   Give a copy to Matt and me.

2. To test whether *me* is correct, omit the words *Matt and.*

   Give a copy to . . . *me*.

Obviously *me* is correct because it's the object of the preposition *to*. Let's look at another example:

1. Read the sentence.

   Ted and I voted against the proposal.

2. Omit the words *Ted and.*

   . . . *I* voted against the proposal.

I is correct because it's the subject of the verb *voted.*

Checkup 7. Underline the correct pronouns.

1. Please let (him, he) and (me, I) do the review.
2. Don't count on Shirley and (I, me) to take the minutes.
3. Should the appointment go to (she, her) or (he, him)?

Check the chart of pronoun forms and uses once again before going on.

Pronouns Following *Than* or *As*. In some sentences, the verb may be stated just once but may also apply to another part of the sentence, even though it is not repeated.

Mr. Lewis gives Marlin more overtime than *me*. Meaning "Mr. Lewis gives Marlin more overtime than *he gives me*." The words *he gives* are understood.

Now look at what happens when we change the pronoun to *I*:

Mr. Lewis gives Marlin more overtime than *I*. Meaning "Mr. Lewis gives Marlin more overtime than *I give Marlin*." Here, the words *give Marlin* are understood.

The reader decides which words are missing by looking at the pronoun that follows the word *than*. A subject pronoun must be the subject of the understood verb. An objective pronoun must be the object of the understood verb.

Following the word *as*, we often find a similar situation:

Does she type as fast as (I, me)?

Which would you choose, *I* or *me*? By completing the sentence, you make the choice an easy one:

Does she type as fast as I *type*? *Type* is the understood verb; *I* is its subject, so *I* is correct.

When you're confronted with a choice of pronouns following *than* or *as*, look for the understood verb. It's mentioned somewhere in the sentence. Then substitute the missing words before you decide which pronoun is correct, the subject form or the objective form.

REVIEW QUIZ

Underline the correct pronouns.

1. Give (we, us) old-timers a chance to see an example.
2. Do all the secretaries but (she, her) take shorthand?
3. Does Andrea swim as well as (me, I)?
4. Show me a sample so that I may judge (its, it's) quality.
5. (Him, He) and (me, I) will stop (them, their) wasting time.
6. They know how to do it as well as (us, we).
7. Divide the files between Richard and (me, I).

8. (Theirs, There's) your copy.
9. No one could be happier than Kent and (I, me).
10. None of the mail is (hers, her's).
11. I know that (him, he) and (me, I) will be accepted.
12. They did not know about (me, my) changing the procedure.
13. Let me know when (your, you're) finished.
14. No one except (we, us) clerks had a paid holiday.
15. Leave the driving to (we, us) experts.

Pronoun Referents and Agreement

REFERENTS

Clear Referents. Proper use of a pronoun depends on having a definite *referent*. A referent is simply the person or thing to which the pronoun refers. If the referent is unclear, the meaning of your sentence will be unclear. For example:

Hal and Ron went into *his* office to discuss *his* promotion.

Whose office and whose promotion? Is the referent Hal, or is it Ron? The sentence needs to be rewritten. To make the referent clear, don't use a pronoun.

Better: **Hal went into his office with Ron to discuss Ron's promotion.**
Or: **Hal and Ron went into Hal's office to discuss Ron's promotion.**

Checkup 1. Rewrite the following sentences so that the referents are clear.

1. Sue and Jill took her typewriter to the repair shop. ______________________

____

2. The teacher and the student met his goal. ______________________

____

3. I knew Stan and Charlie when he was club president. ______________________

____

Self-Ending Pronouns. *Self*-ending pronouns are made by adding *self* or *selves* to a simple pronoun, for example, *himself* or *themselves*. These pronouns must have a referent in the *same* sentence; otherwise a *self*-ending pronoun should not be used. The *self* part of the word indicates that the person has already been mentioned.

REFERENT ↓

***Ann* decorated the office *herself*.**

REFERENT ↓ ↘

***Mrs. LoPinto and Mr. Sayles* made the reservations *themselves*.**

In the following sentences, note that a *self*-ending pronoun cannot be used because there are no referents for *self*-ending pronouns.

Ann gave *me* a haircut. ***Not:*** *gave myself.*
Everett and *I* will contact you. ***Not:*** *and myself.*
They need administrators like *you*. ***Not:*** *like yourselves.*

Checkup 2. Underline the correct pronouns.

1. Harry and (you, yourself) will be on the program.
2. They lost the deal for (them, themselves).
3. I plan to order a filmstrip for (me, myself).
4. Janice and (I, myself) will lead the discussion.

AGREEMENT

A pronoun must not only have a clear referent; it must also *agree with* its referent. Notice how the following pronouns agree with their referents.

SINGULAR		PLURAL	
REFERENT	PRONOUN	REFERENT	PRONOUN
boy	**he, his, him**	**boys**	**them, their, theirs**
girl	**she, her, her**	**girls**	**them, their, theirs**
Carl	**he, his, him**	**Carl and May**	**them, their, theirs**
Betty	**she, her, her**	**Betty and Jim**	**them, their, theirs**
wife	**she, her, her**	**wives**	**them, their, theirs**
husband	**he, his, him**	**husbands**	**them, their, theirs**
desk	**it, its**	**desks**	**them, their, theirs**
house	**it, its**	**houses**	**them, their, theirs**

A singular pronoun is used to agree with a singular noun, and a plural pronoun is used to agree with a plural noun. In addition, only *he, him,* or *his* is used to agree with a singular male noun, and only *she, her,* or *her* is used to agree with a singular female noun.

Singular nouns that show no sex—*desk* and *house*, for example—use *it* and *its*. But the plural pronoun forms are the same; there is no sex distinction in the plural pronouns.

Let's see how the pronouns agree with their referents in the following sentences.

Mrs. Inez forgot *her* watch and had to go back for *it*.

Mr. Halbert said *he* enjoyed *his* vacation.

Male or Female Unknown. A referent such as *manager, teacher, parent, writer,* or *president* can refer to either a man or a woman.

My present manager writes all *her* own letters, but my former manager asked me to write all *his* letters.

Here the writer knows, of course, that *present manager* refers to a female and therefore *her* is correct. The writer also knows that *former manager* is a male and therefore *his* is correct. There is no problem in pronoun reference.

However, sometimes referents such as *manager, teacher,* and so on, are used to refer to *any* manager or *any* teacher. In such cases, you must be sure to make your pronouns agree with the referents as shown in the following examples:

If a customer wishes, *he or she* may exchange any item within ten days of purchase. No specific customer is intended.

A good manager should set *his or her* goals carefully. No specific manager is intended.

Ask each teacher to bring a calculator with *him or her.* No specific teacher is intended.

As you can see, then, for referents such as *a customer, a manager,* or *each teacher,* the correct personal pronoun is often *he or she, his or her,* or *him or her.*

Checkup 3. Revise each sentence as needed.

1. The president of each major corporation has given his help in raising money for this charity. ______________________________

____

2. We will pick the winner today and announce her name at noon tomorrow.

____

3. Every writer knows that he must edit his work carefully. ______________________________

____

4. Each citizen must be sure to cast her vote next Thursday. ______________________________

____

In order to avoid the wordiness of repeating *he or she, his or her,* and *him and her* throughout a message, you may use plural nouns and pronouns. Note how the examples on page 81 can be reworded with plural nouns and pronouns:

If *customers* wish, *they* may . . . .
Good *managers* should set *their* goals . . . .
Ask the *teachers* . . . with *them.*

Checkup 4. Eliminate sex references in each sentence by using plural forms.

1. An applicant should send her résumé to the personnel director. ______________________________

____

2. A typist must concentrate on her work. ______________________________

____

3. If a clerk does not pass the test, we give her a second chance. ______________________________

____

Of course, there are many ways in which sentences can be rewritten to avoid sex bias. Note the following examples:

Each sales representative is given *his or her* annual sales quota by *his or her* district manager. The actual quota assigned to *him or her* depends on the size of *his or her* territory.
Better:
Each marketing representative is given an annual sales quota by the district manager. The actual quota assigned to a representative depends on the size of the territory.

When a customer complains, send *her* to the manager.
Better:
A customer who complains should be sent to the manager.

An effective secretary usually does her work cheerfully.
Better:
An effective secretary usually works cheerfully.

Be creative in finding ways to avoid sex bias in your writing.

Checkup 5. Reword the following sentences to avoid sex bias.

1. Every flight attendant feels tired at the end of her workday. ____________

   ____

2. A considerate employer will treat his employees with respect. ____________

   ____

3. If a teacher succeeds, she is likely to be praised. ____________

   ____

4. The supervisor of a department must not lose his patience. ____________

   ____

5. Each manager was asked to revise his budget by Friday. ____________

   ____

NUMBER AGREEMENT ERRORS

You've already seen that pronouns must agree with their referents in number. Review the singular pronouns and the plural pronouns listed in the chart on page 73. Then study the two common errors made in number agreement.

1. *Their* With a Singular Noun. *Their* is plural, of course, but writers sometimes incorrectly use *their* to agree with singular words such as *company, staff, department,* and *everybody, anybody,* and *anyone.*

   Wrong: **Everybody was asked to submit *their* vacation schedule.**
   Everybody is singular.
   Right: **Everybody was asked to submit *his or her* vacation schedule.**

   Wrong: **Only one of the four supervisors exceeded *their* expense budget.**
   One, the subject of the sentence, is singular.
   Right: **Only one of the four supervisors exceeded *his or her* expense budget.**

   Wrong: **The company has met *their* sales goals for the past ten years.**
   Company is singular.
   Right: **The company has met *its* sales goals for the past ten years.**

2. Referents Joined by *Or* or *Nor.* Referents joined by *and* are plural, of course, and require a plural pronoun.

   Robert and George are planning to announce *their* decision tomorrow.
   Their agrees with *Robert and George.*

But referents joined by *or* (or *nor*) can be tricky. The pronoun must agree with the referent that follows the word *or* (or *nor*):

Robert or George is planning to announce *his* decision tomorrow. *His* agrees with *George*, the word that follows *or.*

Robert or his assistants are planning to announce *their* decision tomorrow. *Their* agrees with *assistants*, the word that follows *or.*

Look for the word that follows *or* and make the pronoun agree with that word. Notice that the verbs in the above sentences also agree with the word that follows *or.*

Checkup 6. Underline the correct pronouns and verbs.

1. Either Pete or his brother (is, are) liable for (his, their) half of the expenses.
2. Shelly and Margaret (ride, rides) (her, their) bikes to work each day.
3. Either the girl or her parents (was, were) asked to volunteer (her, their) time.

In summary: To decide which pronoun is correct, first locate the referent. Then choose a pronoun that agrees in both number and sex.

REVIEW QUIZ

Read the following sentences. If any contains sexist language or confusing pronoun referents, correct the sentence by changing the pronouns or by rewriting the sentence. Write *OK* if a sentence is correct.

1. In most companies, a regional sales manager receives a bonus based on meeting his sales goals. ______________________

   ____

2. A good executive knows that he must motivate his employees. ______________________

   ____

3. As a general rule, a secretary should ask her boss which letter style he prefers. ______________________

   ____

4. A lawyer is responsible for giving his client the best defense available.

   ____

   ____

5. Every citizen should exercise his or her right to vote. ______________________

   ____

6. Michael asked Luke whether he should postpone the project. ______________________

   ____

7. A recent nationwide poll shows that the average head of a household spends approximately 25 percent of his salary on rent or mortgage payments. ______________________________

____

8. Cathy said that Miss Goldstein asked her assistant to help her revise the price list. ______________________________

____

9. If we find a qualified art director, we will hire him immediately. __________

____

10. The medical department has listed a job for a nurse who has her license to practice in our state. ______________________________

____

LESSON 13 Indefinite and Relative Pronouns

INDEFINITE PRONOUNS

As the name *indefinite* suggests, indefinite pronouns do not refer to a definite person, place, or thing. Most indefinite pronouns are singular, but a few are always plural. In addition, one small group of indefinite pronouns may be either singular or plural, depending on the referent.

Singular Indefinite Pronouns. The following words always are singular.

anyone	**everyone**	**no one**	**someone**
anybody	**everybody**	**nobody**	**somebody**
anything	**everything**	**nothing**	**something**
one	**every**	**either**	**another**
each	**each one**	**neither**	**many a**

Singular indefinite pronouns often are used as the subject of a sentence. As a singular subject, the singular indefinite pronoun must be matched with a singular verb and a singular personal pronoun. Note the example on page 86.

Everyone is **expected to do** ***his*** **or** ***her*** **share of the work.**

Since *everyone* is singular and of unknown sex, the singular verb *is* and the singular pronoun *his* or *her* are appropriate. If you have a tendency to think of *everyone* as plural, concentrate on the *one* contained in the word *everyone*. The word really means "every single one"; thus it is singular.

Many a **man** ***has*** **been betrayed by** ***his*** **ambition.**

Since *many a man* is singular and masculine, *has* and *his* are appropriate.

Neither **of the women** ***was*** **present to give** ***her*** **report.**

In a sentence like the one above, be careful to match the verb and the personal pronoun to the actual subject *neither,* not to the noun in the descriptive phrase *of the women* following the subject. The subject is *neither,* not *women*. The phrase *of the women* further identifies the subject *neither.* The phrase *of the women* also tells the reader that the subject is feminine; therefore, *her,* the singular feminine pronoun, is correct.

Checkup 1. Underline the correct pronouns and verbs.

1. Each person must clean (their, his, her, his or her) own work area.
2. Somebody from our staff (has, have) requested that (their, his, her, his or her) sales quota be lowered.
3. Either of the mothers (is, are) ready to volunteer (their, his, her, his or her) services to the charity drive.

Anyone/Everyone. When *anyone* or *everyone* is followed by an *of* phrase, it is written as two words: *any one* or *every one*. In all other cases they are written as one word.

The police searched ***everyone*** **carefully.**
The police searched ***every one*** **of the suspects carefully.** Two words because *every one* is followed by an *of* phrase.

Anyone **could have answered that question.**
Any one **of the managers could have answered that question.** Two words because *any one* is followed by an *of* phrase.

Checkup 2. Underline the correct pronouns.

1. Do you think (anyone, any one) will come?
2. (Anyone, Any one) of the samples will do.
3. We told them to move (everyone, every one) of the boxes.

Plural Indefinite Pronouns. These few indefinite pronouns are always plural.

both **few** **several** **many** **others**

Therefore, they require plural verbs and plural personal pronouns, of course.

Both **men** *were* **aggressive in** *their* **selling.**
Many **policies** *were* **changed after** *they* **were examined.**
Others were **also concerned about** *their* **safety.**

Notice that *many* is always plural, but *many a* is always singular. (The added *a* makes the word refer to just one item.)

Many **jobs** *were* **eliminated by the efficiency expert.**

Many a **job** *was* **eliminated by the efficiency expert.**

Checkup 3. Underline the correct pronouns and verbs.

1. Few communities (has, have) filed (its, their) requests.
2. Many a clerk (has, have) passed (her, his, his or her, their) test.
3. Several of the deliverymen (is, are) changing (his, their) routes.

Singular or Plural Indefinite Pronouns. A few indefinite pronouns can be either singular or plural, depending on the noun to which they refer.

none **any** **some** **more** **most** **all**

A singular referent will make the indefinite pronoun singular, and a plural referent will make the same pronoun plural. In the following examples, note how the referent (in *italic type*) in each sentence determines whether *none, some,* and *all* are singular or plural.

SINGULAR	PLURAL
None of the ***building*** **has been painted.**	**None of the** ***buildings*** **have been painted.**
Some of the ***project*** **has been completed.**	**Some of the** ***projects*** **have been completed.**
All of the ***house*** **is being redecorated.**	**All of the** ***houses*** **are being redecorated.**

As you can see, then, *none, any, some, more, most,* and *all* can be either singular or plural. For these referents, look in the *of* phrase that follows the indefinite pronoun to determine whether the pronoun is singular or plural in a particular sentence.

Checkup 4. Underline the correct pronouns and verbs.

1. It seems that none of the mothers (want, wants) to volunteer (her, their) services.
2. Some of the book (was, were) not printed, because (it, they) (was, were) not checked by the editor.
3. (Has, Have) any of the managers made (his or her, their) reservations yet?
4. Most of the schedules for next year (is, are) not ready yet, because (it, they) must be reviewed by the manufacturing department.

RELATIVE PRONOUNS

Who and *whom* are relative pronouns, as are *whoever* and *whomever.* These four relative pronouns relate to people. Another relative pronoun, *which,* relates to things, while *that* refers to either people or things. Another relative pronoun, *what,* functions alone, without a referent, as in "*What* is wrong?" Since *which, that,* and *what* do not change their form according to how they are used, they seldom cause a problem. The "people pronouns," on the other hand, have *two* forms: *who* and *whom,* and *whoever* and *whomever.*

WHO/WHOM

Who. The subject form of this pronoun is *who*. Either it is used as a subject of a verb or it is used after a linking verb as an identifying word. Remember that linking verbs use subject forms on *both* sides of the linking verb.

SUBJECT VERB

Who as Subject: ***Who* turned off the machine?**

SUBJECT VERB IDENTIFYING WORD

Who as Identifying Word: **It is *who*?**

Checkup 5. Underline the correct relative pronouns.

1. (Who, Whom) volunteered to close the store?
2. I know (who, whom) sent the packages.
3. They asked me (who, whom) it was.
4. (Who, Whom) is the man at the podium?
5. Do you know (who, whom) is scheduled to follow Ms. Parks?

Whom. The objective form of *who* is *whom.* As with the objective form of any noun or pronoun, *whom* can be used as the object of a verb or as the object of a preposition.

	OBJECT ↓ VERB ↓
Object of Verb:	They asked *whom* we preferred.
	PREPOSITION ↓ OBJECT ↓
Object of Preposition:	I don't know *with whom* he traveled.

Checkup 6. Underline the correct relative pronouns.

1. Find out for (who, whom) he works.
2. To (who, whom) was the letter addressed?
3. I do not know (who, whom) he represents.
4. With (who, whom) did Mrs. Manley go to lunch?

Identifying the Relative Clause. You saw that *who* is used as a subject and *whom* is used as an object. Let's compare *who/whom* to *he/him.* You know that *he* is a subject and *him* is an object, and you know when *he* is correct and when *him* is correct. Now remember that *who* is a subject and *whom* is an object. Then test your sentence by substituting *he.* If *he* would be correct, then *who* would be correct. If *him* would be correct, then *whom* is your choice. In other words:

HE = WHO
HI*M* – WHO*M* (Note the *m* in each word.)

Use this four-step procedure to help you choose between *who* and *whom*:

1. Find the relative clause containing *who* or *whom* and separate it from the rest of the sentence. (Leave the main sentence as it is.)
2. Make certain that the parts of the clause are in normal sentence order, that is, the subject is followed by the verb.
3. Substitute *he* or *him* where *who* or *whom* belongs to see whether you need a subject or an object.
4. If *he* is correct in the sentence, choose *who;* if *him* is correct, choose *whom.*

Let's apply these four steps to this sentence:

The person to (who, whom) I spoke was pleasant.

1. Separate the clause:

   to (who, whom) I spoke
   The person **was pleasant.**

   Notice that the rest of the sentence makes sense without the relative clause.

2. Arrange the clause in normal order:

   SUBJECT ↓ VERB ↓
   I spoke to (who, whom)

3. Substitute *he, him*:

I spoke to (~~he~~, him)

4. Replace *who* or *whom*:

The person **to whom I spoke** **was pleasant.**

In step 3 you see that *him* is correct in the sentence; thus *whom* is the proper relative pronoun. Both are object forms. You can be sure of this choice by noticing that *whom* is the object of the preposition *to*. Now let's try another example:

The executive (who, whom) just came in is famous.

1. Separate the clause:

The executive **(who, whom) just came in** **is famous.**

2. Already in normal order:

SUBJECT ↓ (who, ~~whom~~) — VERB ↓ came

(who, ~~whom~~) just came in.

3. Substitute *he, him*:

(he, ~~him~~) just came in.

Since *he* is correct, *who* is correct. Both are subject forms.

4. Replace *who* or *whom*:

The executive **who just came in** **is famous.**

Finding the relative clause is sometimes tricky. The structure of a sentence may make it hard to tell exactly where the relative clause starts and ends. As a clause, it must have both a subject and a verb. But other extra words can sometimes interrupt the *who/whom* clause.

In the following sentences, note that the interrupters (*in italics*) do not affect the choice of *who* or *whom*.

Anne is the person **who *we think* is going to win.**

The applicant **whom *he feels* he should select** **will be here later.**

In choosing *who* or *whom*, be sure to ignore such interrupting expressions. In the first sentence above, *who* is correct; it is the subject of the verb *is going*. In the second sentence, *whom* is correct; it is the object of the verb *should select* (*should select him, should select whom*).

Review the four-step procedure for choosing between *who* and *whom* to make sure that you can apply it easily.

Checkup 7. Underline the correct relative pronouns.

1. I wonder (who, whom) will be chosen.
2. She knew (who, whom) I was.
3. Merit raises will be given to those people (who, whom) have been the most productive.
4. This is the candidate (who, whom) we want.
5. We forgot (who, whom) it was.

WHOEVER/WHOMEVER

The pronoun *whoever* is a subject form, and *whomever* is an object form. The choice between *whoever* and *whomever* can be made in almost the same way you decided about *who* and *whom.* Try substituting *he* for *whoever* and *him* for *whomever.* It's a little more tricky than that, but let's start there.

You should give it to (whoever, whomever) arrives first.

1. Separate the relative clause, making sure you have both a subject and a verb.

   VERB ↓
   (whoever, whomever) arrives first.

2. The clause is already in normal order.
3. Substitute *he* or *him.*

   (he, ~~him~~) arrives first.

4. Replace *he* with *whoever.*

   You should give it to *whoever* arrives first.

Why do we separate *who/whom* clauses and *whoever/whomever* clauses from the rest of the sentence? Because whether these pronouns are subjects or objects depends on their use *within* these clauses. The rest of the sentence has no effect on whether a subject form or an object form is needed. Look at this example:

You should give it to **whoever arrives first.**

Whoever is not the object of the preposition *to.* The entire clause is the object of the preposition *to*! Within the clause, *whoever* functions as the subject of the verb *arrives.* That's why *whoever* (not *whomever*) is correct in this sentence. Now you know why it's important to separate the *who/whom* clause or *whoever/whomever* clause from the rest of the sentence.

Checkup 8. Underline the correct pronouns.

1. (Whoever, Whomever) finds the key should return it to the receptionist.
2. You may ask (whoever, whomever) you wish to ask.
3. We should talk to (whoever, whomever) is responsible.

WHO OR *WHOM* IN QUESTIONS

The choice between *who* and *whom* in questions can be made simply by answering the question using *he* or *him*. Again *he* = *who* and *him* = *whom*.

Question: **(Who, Whom) did you speak to?**
Answer: **I spoke to (he, him).**
Substitute Whom for Him: ***Whom*** **did you speak to?**

Question: **(Who, Whom) shall we say called?**
Answer: **We shall say (he, him) called.**
Substitute Who for He: ***Who*** **shall we say called?**

Question: **(Who, Whom) was it?**
Answer: **It was** ***he.*** (Remember that a linking verb takes a subject form pronoun!)
Substitute Who for He: ***Who*** **was it?**

Checkup 9. Underline the correct pronouns.

1. (Who, Whom) is the new secretary-treasurer?
2. To (who, whom) will the newsletter be mailed?
3. (Who, Whom) made these mistakes?

Go back and quickly review the examples in this lesson. Remember the key: *Who* is a subject, and *whom* is an object.

REVIEW QUIZ

Underline the correct pronouns and verbs.

1. (Who, Whom) did you expect to answer?
2. To (who, whom) is the letter addressed?
3. The report is intended for (whoever, whomever) is interested.
4. (Whoever, Whomever) plans to attend should respond by July 1.
5. Everyone (who, whom) works late will be paid overtime.
6. Both of the soldiers (is, are, am) going to (his, her, his or her, their) quarters.
7. Is she the candidate (who, whom) you selected?
8. The caller, (whoever, whomever) she was, left no message.
9. Many a company (has, have) had (its, it's, their) tax problems handled by our firm.
10. Call and give the order to the salesperson (who, whom) answers.
11. Address the letter to (whoever, whomever) is on the list.
12. Some of the statements you made (is, are) controversial.

13. The delegates forgot (who, whom) elected them.
14. (Everyone, Every one) of the women (want, wants) to give (her, their) speech first.
15. Help will be welcomed from (whoever, whomever) will give it.

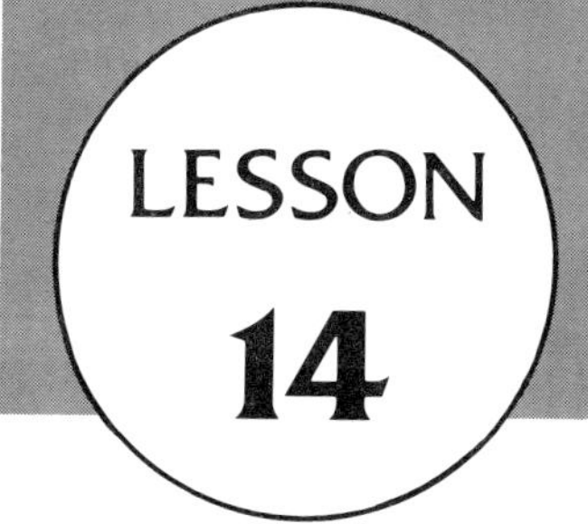

LESSON 14

SECTION 4 WRAP-UP: Pronouns

It's time to review pronouns to prepare for a spelling quiz. Be sure to check back in the lessons if you have questions.

PRONOUN REMINDERS

The following statements are reminders of common, irritating mistakes found in everyday business communications. Do your best to avoid them!

Error: **When the caller asked for Ms. Bronson, I answered, "This is *her*."**

Remember that linking verbs such as *is, was,* and *were* act like an equals sign (=). The pronoun on either side of the sign must be a subject pronoun.

Correction: **When the caller asked for Ms. Bronson, I answered, "This is *she*."**

Error: **Ask him to give a copy to you and *I*.**

Both of these pronouns (*you* and *I*) are objects of the preposition *to*, so both must be in the objective form.

Correction: **Ask him to give a copy to you and *me*.** Meaning "*to* you and *to* me."

Error: **You may send the application to *myself*.**

A *self*-ending pronoun must have a referent in the *same* sentence. In the sentence above, *myself* has no referent; thus *me* is correct.

Correction: **You may send the application to *me*.**

Error: **Everyone went *their* own way.**

Pronouns must agree with their referents in both number and sex. *Their* does not agree with singular referents such as *everyone, someone, each,* and *every.* Change *their* to *his or her* or rewrite the sentence.

Correction: **Everyone went *his or her* own way.**
Or: **All of the participants went *their* own way.**

Error: **I read *everyone* of the pages.**

When words such as *everyone* and *anyone* are followed by an *of* phrase, they are spelled as two words.

Correction: **I read *every one* of the pages.**

SPELLING EXERCISE

1. Correct all misspelled words in the following list. Place a C after words that are already correctly spelled. Be ready for a spelling quiz.
2. Write an appropriate pronoun for each word in the space provided at the right, as in the example.

WORD	CORRECT SPELLING	APPROPRIATE PRONOUN
0. existense	existence	it
1. funcshun		
2. labratory		
3. amature		
4. surgeon		
5. principel		
6. principal		
7. parlament		
8. rooteens		
9. psycology		
10. vacume		
11. capitols		
12. capatol		
13. chauffer		
14. pnumonia		
15. morgage		

SECTION 5

Modifiers and Connectives

YOUR GOALS

After finishing this section, you will be able to:

1. Correctly form comparative and superlative adjectives.
2. Choose the correct adjectives to (a) compare two items and (b) compare three or more items.
3. Use *a* and *an* correctly.
4. Recognize the uses of adjectives and adverbs.
5. Master the most common troublesome adjectives and adverbs and use them correctly.
6. Correctly use the most common troublesome prepositions and conjunctions.
7. Correctly spell and change to adverbs 15 commonly misspelled adjectives.

LESSON 15 Adjectives

So far we've concentrated on the major parts of a sentence: subjects (nouns and pronouns) and verbs. The subject and the verb provide the skeleton of a sentence, but other words, such as modifiers and connectives, do affect the "shape" of our message. *Modifiers* are explanatory or descriptive words that tell more about some other word or words in the sentence. *Adjectives* and *adverbs* are modifiers. *Connectives* are words that join parts of the sentence to tie the message together. *Prepositions* and *conjunctions* are connectives.

In this lesson you'll learn about one kind of modifier—*adjectives*.

ADJECTIVES

Adjectives are descriptive words that tell something about a noun, such as its color, number, kind, size, and so on.

green **room** *six* **offices** *rich* **woman** *large* **house**

Notice how the following nouns are described by two or more adjectives:

my new **apartment** *expensive, gaudy* **furniture**
their revised **estimate** *practical, simple* **clothing**

As you see, the pronouns *my* and *their* are adjectives when they describe nouns, as they do in the examples above. Also, you may have noticed that *revised* comes from the verb *revise*, but *revised* is an adjective here because it, too, describes a noun. Words that describe nouns are adjectives.

Checkup 1. Underline the adjectives.

1. They hired two young women to run our regional offices.
2. His black chair matches his black bookcase.
3. We adopted her excellent system for filing new contracts.

KINDS OF ADJECTIVES

Adjectives can be descriptive, comparative, or superlative.

Descriptive Adjectives. Descriptive adjectives describe one item or group of items, without making a comparison.

new **contract** *early* **meeting** *hard* **task**

Comparative Adjectives. Comparative adjectives show more or less of a given quality as compared to another item. In other words, they show *comparisons.* Most comparative adjectives are formed by adding *er* to the descriptive adjective.

Descriptive: **This is a *clean* room.** No comparison is made.
Comparative: **Dan's room is *cleaner* than Rick's room.** Compares two rooms.

Descriptive: **She is a *rich* woman.** No comparison is made.
Comparative: **She is the *richer* woman of the two.** Compares two women.

Checkup 2. Provide comparative forms of the following adjectives.

1. hard ____________
2. soft ____________
3. tight ____________
4. small ____________

Superlative Adjectives. Notice the word *super* in *superlative. Superlative* means "the most," and superlative adjectives are used to compare three or more items. Superlatives are usually formed by adding *est* to the descriptive adjective.

Descriptive: **Mrs. Temple is a *rich* woman.** No comparison is made.
Superlative: **Mrs. Temple is the *richest* of the four women.** Compares four women.

Descriptive: **Frank's office is *clean.*** No comparison is made.
Superlative: **Frank's is the *cleanest* of all six offices.** Compares six offices.

Caution: Do not use the superlative form when comparing only two items. (Not: *cleanest* of the two rooms or *richest* of the two women.)

Checkup 3. Provide superlative forms of the following adjectives.

1. poor ____________
2. dark ____________
3. cruel ____________
4. light ____________

ADJECTIVES WITH *MORE* AND *MOST*

As mentioned before, most comparative and superlative adjectives are formed by adding *er* and *est*. But some adjectives would become very hard (or impossible!) to pronounce if *er* or *est* were added. For example, can you imagine saying "ridiculouser" and "ridiculousest"? Of course not! Therefore, we often use *more* and *most* (or *less* and *least*) together with the descriptive adjective to show the comparative and superlative forms.

Descriptive: **This is a *difficult* problem.**
Comparative: **This is a *more* difficult problem than that one.**
Superlative: **This is the *most* difficult problem of all.**

Descriptive: **Kelly is *patient*.**
Comparative: **Judd is *less* patient than Kelly.**
Superlative: **Ken is the *least* patient of the three.**

Checkup 4. Provide comparative and superlative forms of the following adjectives using both *more/most* and *less/least*.

DESCRIPTIVE		COMPARATIVE		SUPERLATIVE
1. regular	a.	______	a.	______
	b.	______	b.	______
2. fantastic	a.	______	a.	______
	b.	______	b.	______
3. unsatisfactory	a.	______	a.	______
	b.	______	b.	______
4. profitable	a.	______	a.	______
	b.	______	b.	______
5. practical	a.	______	a.	______
	b.	______	b.	______

How do you know which adjectives use *er* and *est* and which use *more/most* and *less/least*? You can tell by the way the form sounds. Most one-syllable adjectives just add *er* and *est* and are easy to pronounce. On the other hand, adjectives with three or more syllables cannot add *er* or *est*. They need *more/most* or *less/least*. (You saw the reason when you tried to pronounce "ridiculouser" and "ridiculousest.")

Two-Syllable Adjectives. Adjectives with two syllables can either add *er/est* or use *more/most* and *less/least*.

DESCRIPTIVE	COMPARATIVE	SUPERLATIVE
hungry	**hungri*er***	**hungri*est***
lovely	**loveli*er***	**loveli*est***
lovely	***more* lovely**	***most* lovely**
	***less* lovely**	***least* lovely**

Checkup 5. Provide comparative and superlative forms of the following adjectives using both *more/most* and *less/least*.

DESCRIPTIVE		COMPARATIVE		SUPERLATIVE
1. ragged	a.	______________	a.	______________
	b.	______________	b.	______________
2. prejudiced	a.	______________	a.	______________
	b.	______________	b.	______________
3. believable	a.	______________	a.	______________
	b.	______________	b.	______________
4. progressive	a.	______________	a.	______________
	b.	______________	b.	______________
5. serious	a.	______________	a.	______________
	b.	______________	b.	______________

SPELLING OF COMPARATIVE AND SUPERLATIVE ADJECTIVES

Words formed by adding *er* and *est* follow several of the same spelling rules we have already discussed for nouns and verbs. Let's review.

Adjectives Ending in a Vowel Plus *Y*. When adding *er* or *est* to an adjective ending in a vowel plus *y*, keep the *y*.

VOWEL ↓

gray **grayer** (↑ KEEP *y*) **grayest** (↑ KEEP *y*)

Adjectives Ending in a Consonant Plus *Y*. Before adding *er* or *est* to an adjective ending in a consonant plus *y*, change the *y* to *i*.

CONSONANT ↓

pretty **prettier** (↑ CHANGE *y* TO *i*) **prettiest** (↑ CHANGE *y* TO *i*)

Checkup 6. Provide comparative and superlative forms of the following adjectives.

DESCRIPTIVE		COMPARATIVE		SUPERLATIVE
1. silly	1.	______________	1.	______________
2. funny	2.	______________	2.	______________
3. muddy	3.	______________	3.	______________

Adjectives Ending in a Single Vowel Plus a Single Consonant. Before adding *er* and *est* to an adjective ending in a single vowel plus a single consonant, double the consonant.

VOWEL
CONSONANT

fat	**fatter**	**fattest**
	DOUBLE CONSONANT	DOUBLE CONSONANT

Checkup 7. Provide comparative and superlative forms of the following adjectives.

DESCRIPTIVE	COMPARATIVE	SUPERLATIVE
1. thin	1. ______	1. ______
2. red	2. ______	2. ______
3. mad	3. ______	3. ______

IRREGULAR ADJECTIVES

The comparative and superlative forms of a few familiar adjectives are formed irregularly. Look at these special forms:

DESCRIPTIVE	COMPARATIVE	SUPERLATIVE
bad, ill	**worse**	**worst**
good, well	**better**	**best**
far	**farther, further**	**farthest, furthest**
late	**later, latter**	**latest, last**
little	**littler, less, lesser**	**littlest, least**
much, many	**more**	**most**

Checkup 8. Underline the correct adjectives.

1. Fannie does (gooder, better) work than Kate.
2. She has the (baddest, worse, worst) filing system in the building.
3. Although I have many books, she has (manyer, more, most).

ARTICLES

The words *the, a,* and *an* are special adjectives used to identify nouns. These words are called *articles.*

Indefinite and Definite Articles. *A* and *an* are indefinite articles. They do not identify a specific item. *The* is a definite article because it does refer to a specific item.

Indefinite: **Tell me *a* story.** Any story.
Give me *an* eraser. Any eraser.

Definite: **Tell me *the* story.** A specific story.
Give me *the* eraser. A specific eraser.

Checkup 9. Underline the correct articles.

1. Send me (a, the) memo you got from Hadley yesterday.
2. Let's meet in (a, the) conference room next to my office.
3. I usually eat (a, the) light lunch.

Choice Between *A* and *An*. The choice between *a* and *an* is made according to the *sound* (not necessarily the spelling) of the word following *a* or *an*. *A* is used before a consonant sound and *an* before a vowel sound (*a, e, i, o, u*).

***A* BEFORE CONSONANTS**	***AN* BEFORE VOWELS**
CONSONANTS	VOWELS
***a* car** ***a* bush**	***an* apple** ***an* invitation**

Checkup 10. Write *a* or *an*, whichever is correct.

1. ___ basket 2. ___ elevator 3. ___ message 4. ___ error

Special Cases. The letters *f* and *h* are consonants, but they may sometimes be pronounced as vowels. On the other hand, the letters *o* and *u* are vowels, but they may sometimes be pronounced as consonants. Let's see examples of each situation:

	CONSONANT SOUND	VOWEL SOUND
F:	***a* fact**	***an* FHA loan** ("ef")
H:	***a* house**	***an* hour** ("ow")
O:	***a* one-year license** ("w")	***an* onion**
U:	***a* unit** ("y")	***an* ulcer**

Checkup 11. Write *a* or *an*, whichever is correct.

1. ___ habit 3. ___ ukulele 5. ___ uncle 7. ___ fire
2. ___ f.o.b. order 4. ___ one-way street 6. ___ honor 8. ___ office

FEWER AND *LESS*

The comparative adjectives *fewer* and *less* are often misused. *Fewer* means "not as *many*," while *less* means "not as *much*."

Fewer. *Fewer* refers to *number* of things (items that can be counted) and is used with *plural* nouns.

We drove *fewer miles* than they did. Meaning "not as *many*" miles.

Less. *Less* refers to total *amount* or degree and is used with *singular* nouns.

We used *less gas* than they did. Meaning "not as *much*" gas.

Checkup 12. Write *fewer* or *less,* whichever is correct.

1. There are ________________ mistakes in this report.
2. We showed ________________ profit than ever.
3. Make ________________ copies than you made yesterday.
4. Because the Hilltop Hotel had ________________ conference rooms, we could not hold our meetings there.
5. Since we now have all the inventory information on computers, we can prepare the annual inventory in ________________ time.

REVIEW QUIZ

Underline the correct adjectives.

1. This is the (better, best) copy machine I've ever seen.
2. We will be ready in (a, an) few minutes.
3. She parked the car on (a, an) one-way street.
4. Which bread has (less, fewer) calories?
5. I interviewed two applicants, and I hired the (better, best) one.
6. She will receive (an, a) honorary degree from Harvard.
7. Which of the pair has the (brighter, brightest) color?
8. They have had (less, fewer) trouble with the engine since it was repaired.
9. We will have (more, most) time later than now.
10. Andrea is (beautifuller, more beautiful) than Sandra.
11. (A, An) umbrella would be handy today.
12. I'll take (the, a) biggest box.
13. Irv Hill is (an, a) honest, reliable mechanic.
14. Which of your feet is (less, least) sore?
15. (An, A) FHA loan is (a, an) federally guaranteed loan.
16. Tina is the (lazier, laziest) of the twins.
17. Carl is the (sensitivist, most sensitive) person in our entire office.
18. We will have (fewer, less) problems when we get the new computer.
19. I always read the (latter, last) page of a mystery first.
20. She attended (a, an) university on the West Coast.

Adverbs

Like adjectives, adverbs are also descriptive words. However, adverbs don't modify nouns. (Only adjectives do that.) Rather, adverbs modify verbs, adjectives, or other adverbs. They tell Where? How? When? How much? or To what degree?

Look at some common adverbs:

You may put the box ***there.*** Tells where.
Mrs. Ryan dictates ***rapidly.*** Tells how.
We will get a raise *soon.* Tells when.
We cleaned our room ***thoroughly.*** Tells to what degree.

FORMING *LY* ADVERBS

Most adverbs end in *ly*. Let's see how easy it is to form *ly* adverbs.

From Most Adjectives. Most adverbs are formed by simply adding *ly* to an adjective.

Adjective:	**rapid**	**shrewd**	**immediate**
Adverb:	**rapid*ly***	**shrewd*ly***	**immediate*ly***

Checkup 1. Form adverbs from these adjectives.

1. quick ______________________ 3. sure ______________________
2. warm ______________________ 4. high ______________________

From Adjectives Ending in *LL*. For adjectives that end in *ll*, simply add *y* to form the adverb.

Adjective:	**shrill**	**full**	**dull**
Adverb:	**shrill*y***	**full*y***	**dull*y***

From Adjectives Ending in *LE*. For adjectives ending in *le*, change the *e* to *y*.

Adjective:	**comfortable**	**reasonable**
Adverb:	**comfortabl*y***	**reasonabl*y***

Checkup 2. Form adverbs from these adjectives.

1. simple ______________________ 3. indelible ______________________
2. possible ______________________ 4. miserable ______________________

From Adjectives Ending in *Y*. For adjectives ending in *y*, change the *y* to *i* and add *ly*.

Adjective:	**busy**	**satisfactory**
Adverb:	**bus*i*l*y***	**satisfactor*i*l*y***
	CHANGE *y* TO *i*	CHANGE *y* TO i

Checkup 3. Form adverbs from these adjectives.

1. easy ______________________ 3. temporary ______________________
2. ready ______________________ 4. necessary ______________________

Exceptions: Several very common adverbs do not follow these rules. Memorize these one-syllable *e*-ending adjectives and their irregular adverb forms.

Adjective:	**due**	**true**	**whole**
Adverb:	**duly**	**truly**	**wholly**

OTHER ADVERBS

Many adverbs have distinct forms of their own.

almost	**already**	**also**	**always**	**away**	**well**
here	**much**	**never**	**now**	**once**	**twice**
quite	**rather**	**somewhat**	**soon**	**then**	**still**
there	**together**	**too**	**very**		

Checkup 4. Underline the adverbs.

1. This is a very interesting report.
2. They threw away the first draft of the contract.
3. Our staff has already decided that there is too much work.

CHOOSING BETWEEN ADJECTIVES AND ADVERBS

The choice between using an adjective or an adverb in a sentence depends upon the word modified. ***Remember:*** Adjectives modify only nouns or pronouns. Adverbs never modify nouns or pronouns; they modify verbs, adjectives, or other adverbs. As you know, the *ly* ending usually signals that the modifier is an adverb. Compare the uses of these adjectives and adverbs.

ADJECTIVE NOUN

Adjective: **She is a *careful* typist.**

Careful modifies the noun *typist*.

VERB ADVERB

Adverb: **She types *carefully*.**

Carefully modifies the verb *types*. Types how? *Carefully*.

ADJECTIVE NOUN

Adjective: **They serve *real* cream.**

Real modifies the noun *cream*.

ADVERB ADJECTIVE NOUN

Adverb: **They serve *really* big portions.**

Really modifies the adjective *big*, and *big* modifies the noun *portions*. How big? *Really* big.

ADJECTIVE NOUN

Adjective: **It is a *sure* investment.**

Sure modifies the noun *investment*.

ADVERB VERB

Adverb: **It *surely* will result in a profit.**

Surely modifies the verb phrase *will result* and tells to what degree.

ADJECTIVE NOUN

Adjective: **This is a *clear* picture.**

Clear modifies the noun *picture*.

ADVERB
ADJECTIVE

Adverb: **This is *clearly* wrong.**

Clearly modifies the adjective *wrong*.

Checkup 5. Underline the correct adjective or adverb. Then underline the word it modifies.

1. I (sure, surely) agree with Ms. Hobson's suggestions.
2. Return these files (careful, carefully).
3. Jackie is a (sure, surely) winner.
4. It was a (real, really) exciting game.
5. I never saw a more (careful, carefully) person.
6. The representative (clear, clearly) explained how to use the product.
7. They import only (real, really) antiques.
8. A (clear, clearly) answer is needed.

After Linking Verbs. As you remember, linking verbs such as *seem/seems, feel/feels*, and so on, can be replaced by *is* or *are* without changing the meaning of the message. On the other hand, if the verb can't be replaced by *is* or *are*, it is an action verb, not a linking verb. Let's review this usage.

LINKING VERB
ADJECTIVE

Linking Verb: **He *looks* quick.** (Meaning "He *is* quick.")

Because *looks* can be replaced by *is*, *looks* is a linking verb that joins the descriptive adjective *quick* to *he*, the pronoun it modifies.

ACTION VERB ADVERB

Action Verb: **He looks at the papers *quickly*.**

"He *is* at the papers" makes no sense. Because *looks* cannot be replaced by *is* in this sentence, *looks* is an action verb that is modified by *quickly*. *Quickly* is an adverb telling How?

Once you know whether you are dealing with a linking verb or an action verb, you easily can decide whether to use an adjective or an adverb. Use adjectives to modify nouns or pronouns, and use adjectives (not adverbs) after linking verbs. Use adverbs to modify verbs, adjectives, or other adverbs—that is, use adverbs to tell How? When? Where? How much? or To what degree?

LINKING VERB
ADJECTIVE

Adjective: **He felt *strong*.**

Strong follows a linking verb; therefore, it is an adjective describing *he*.

ACTION VERB ADVERB

Adverb: **He felt the material *carefully*.**

Carefully is an adverb describing the *action* of feeling. It answers the question How?

LINKING VERB ADJECTIVE

Adjective: **Our manager looked *different* this morning.**

Different follows a linking verb; therefore, it is an adjective describing the noun *manager.*

ACTION VERB ADVERB

Adverb: **Our manager looked at the possibilities *differently* today.**

Differently is an adverb describing the *action* of looking. It answers the question How?

Checkup 6. Underline the correct adjective or adverb. Then underline the word it modifies.

1. The situation looked (different, differently) after a week.
2. Your department is (sure, surely) active.
3. Ms. Garcia felt (happy, happily) about her promotion.

Bad/Badly. Do you ever wonder whether to use *good* or *well* or *bad* or *badly* in a sentence? A lot of people do. Let's look at the uses of these tricky adjectives and adverbs.

bad: **always an adjective**
badly: **always an adverb (note the *ly*)**
good: **always an adjective**
well: **either an adjective (referring to health) or an adverb (telling How?)**

If you remember that linking verbs require an adjective and that action verbs require an adverb, you'll choose *bad* after linking verbs and *badly* after action verbs.

LINKING VERB ADJECTIVE

Adjective Following a Linking Verb: **I feel *bad*.**

Bad is an identifying adjective following a linking verb. *Bad* describes the pronoun *I*.

ACTION VERB ADVERB

Adverb Following an Action Verb: **I play the piano *badly*.**

Badly is an adverb describing the *action* of playing. It tells How?

Checkup 7. Underline the correct adjective or adverb. Then underline the word it modifies.

1. She performed (bad, badly) at the concert.
2. I think they felt (bad, badly) about canceling the luncheon.
3. This coffee tastes (bad, badly), doesn't it?

Good/Well. Since *good* is always an adjective, *good* must describe a noun or pronoun.

ADJECTIVE
NOUN

Before a Noun: **That was a *good* move.**

LINKING VERB
ADJECTIVE

Following a Linking Verb: **Our chances seem *good.***

Well is usually an adverb telling How?

ACTION VERB
ADVERB

Adverb Following an Action Verb: **You scored *well* on all the tests.**

Well modifies the verb *scored*; therefore, *well* is an adverb.

ADVERB ADJECTIVE

Adverb Modifying an Adjective: **They were *well* prepared.**

Well modifies the adjective *prepared*; therefore, *well* is an adverb.

But *well* also can be used as an adjective *only* when describing health.

LINKING VERB
ADJECTIVE

Theresa looks *well.*

You've seen that an adjective is needed after a linking verb. Just remember that instead of the adjective *good* you must substitute *well* in only *one* case: when you're referring to health. In all other cases, *well* is an adverb. (***Hint:*** Remember that *well-being* means health, and you'll remember that *well* is the adjective to use when referring to health.)

Checkup 8. Underline the correct adjective or adverb.

1. The staff meeting was (good, well) attended.
2. You know a (good, well) opportunity when you see it.
3. Thomas looks (good, well) since his surgery.

4. She is (good, well) to her employees.
5. This spaghetti tastes (good, well).
6. They all work (good, well) together.
7. All of us agreed that the advertising campaign was planned very (good, well).

REVIEW QUIZ

Underline the correct adjective or adverb. Then underline the word it modifies. Also, identify each choice by writing *adj* or *adv* in the space following each sentence. An example is given.

0.	He does not play the piano (good, well).	0. adv
1.	We must check these figures (accurate, accurately).	1. ______
2.	The house looked (different, differently) in the moonlight.	2. ______
3.	It's a (clear, clearly) case of fraud.	3. ______
4.	I don't feel (good, well) since I had the flu.	4. ______
5.	Helen bought a (real, really) antique.	5. ______
6.	I hope you don't feel (bad, badly) about the postponement.	6. ______
7.	When the project was finished successfully, we felt (good, well).	7. ______
8.	The race is a (sure, surely) thing.	8. ______
9.	That movie was (real, really) long.	9. ______
10.	She had her hair styled (different, differently).	10. ______
11.	This perfume smells (bad, badly).	11. ______
12.	My assistant always dresses (casual, casually).	12. ______
13.	The project will (sure, surely) be delayed.	13. ______
14.	We walked into an (elegant, elegantly) decorated room.	14. ______
15.	We (sure, surely) were busy.	15. ______
16.	Marlene works (good, well) under pressure.	16. ______
17.	Our coach always feels (bad, badly) when we lose.	17. ______
18.	The brochures were (poor, poorly) printed.	18. ______
19.	His office was damaged (bad, badly).	19. ______
20.	They walked (slow, slowly).	20. ______

Prepositions

PREPOSITIONS AND THEIR OBJECTS

Prepositions are connectives. They are familiar words that link a noun or pronoun to the rest of the sentence. Here are some commonly used prepositions:

about	**above**	**across**	**after**	**against**
among	**around**	**before**	**behind**	**below**
beneath	**between**	**beyond**	**but**	**by**
down	**during**	**for**	**from**	**except**
in	**into**	**of**	**off**	**on**
concerning	**regarding**	**respecting**	**onto**	**since**
through	**throughout**	**till**	**to**	**toward**
under	**underneath**	**until**	**up**	**upon**
with	**within**	**without**		

Notice the parts of the word *pre/position. Pre* means "before" (as in *preheat, prepaid, pretax*) and *position* means "place." As you'll see, prepositions are words that are placed *before* nouns and pronouns. The nouns and pronouns that follow prepositions are called *objects of prepositions.* In the following examples, the objects of the prepositions are in *italics.*

near *him*	**to** *them*	**with** *her*
after *work*	**in** *Chicago*	**for** *Carl*

Checkup 1. Underline the objects of the prepositions.

1. We left after lunch.
2. They agreed with him.
3. Is he in trouble?
4. Her office is below mine.

PREPOSITIONAL PHRASES

Sometimes, the objects of prepositions may have modifiers.

into the garage (*the* modifies *garage*)
in our new office (*our* and *new* modify *office*)
for her former boss (*her* and *former* modify *boss*)

And sometimes there may be two or more objects:

between ***you*** **and** ***me*** (*and* connects the two objects, *you, me*)
for ***Jack, Bill,*** **or** ***me*** (*or* connects three objects, *Jack, Bill, me*)

Together, a preposition, its object (or objects), and any modifiers form a *prepositional phrase.* As you'll see from the prepositional phrases in the following sentences, by itself each phrase does *not* give the reader a complete thought. However, each phrase does show a relationship to some other part of the sentence.

He hit the ball ***toward my brother.*** *Toward my brother* shows direction.
She went shopping ***during lunch hour.*** *During lunch hour* indicates time.
We sat ***near Mrs. Shipley.*** *Near Mrs. Shipley* shows position.

Checkup 2. Underline the prepositional phrases and circle the objects.

1. We finished early in the evening.
2. Put the order on our account.
3. We went into the office before lunch.
4. During March and April all our regional managers will be planning next year's budget.
5. Everyone received a copy except John.

Note that some prepositions consist of more than one word.

because of	**along with**	**as to**	**out of**
from beyond	**contrary to**	**by way of**	**in front of**
in accordance with	**in addition to**	**in place of**	**in spite of**
in view of	**on account of**	**with respect to**	

TROUBLESOME PREPOSITIONS

A few prepositions may be troublesome. Pay special attention to these troublemakers.

Between/Among. *Between* is used to show a relationship involving *two* items. *Among* is used to show a relationship involving *three or more* items.

This news is just *between* you and me. Two people.
We will divide the profit *among* the five of us. Three or more people.

Checkup 3. Underline the correct preposition.

1. The choice is (between, among) these two samples.
2. Distribute the copies (between, among) the four department heads.
3. The contest wasn't (between, among) the two managers but (between, among) all of the employees.

***Different From* (Not *Different Than*).** *Different* is used with *from,* not with *than.*

My contract is *different from* yours. ***Not:*** *different than yours.*

***Retroactive To* (Not *Retroactive From*).** *Retroactive* is used with *to,* not with *from.*

Our cost-of-living raise was *retroactive to* July 1. ***Not:*** *retroactive from July 1.*

Checkup 4. Underline the correct preposition.

1. Will the increase be retroactive (to, from) January 1?
2. Why is my agenda different (than, from) yours?
3. This carbon copy is different (than, from) the original.
4. Tax rebates are never retroactive (from, to) an earlier date.

In/Into/In To. *In* means "to be within." *Into* means "to move from outside to inside—to enter." *In to* is two words, an adverb (*in*) plus a preposition (*to*).

Mrs. Pike is *in* the living room. Within.
Let's move quickly *into* the room. Moving from outside to inside.
They brought the request *in to* Ray. Adverb plus preposition.

Checkup 5. Underline the correct preposition.

1. They jumped (in, into, in to) the pool.
2. Mr. Curtis is (in, into, in to) his office now.
3. They all went (in, into, in to) dinner.

Angry With/Angry At. *Angry at* is used when referring to things, and *angry with* is used when referring to people.

I am angry *at* the work. At a thing.
I am angry *with* you. With a person.

***Have* (Not *Of*).** *Of* should not be used in place of *have* in phrases such as *should have, would have,* and *must have.*

We should *have* attended the conference. *Not: should of.*

Checkup 6. Underline the correct choices.

1. I don't think he should (of, have) been angry (at, with) them.
2. It's no use getting angry (at, with) the weather.
3. Your supervisor must (of, have) been very angry (at, with) you.

***Behind* (Not *In Back Of*).** *In back of* should not be used in place of *behind.*

The coat rack is *behind* the door. *Not: in back of the door.*

***Off* (Not *Off of* or *Off From*).** *Off* should not be coupled with *of* or *from. Off* already tells us what happened. The extra prepositions *of* and *from* are unnecessary words that don't add any information.

The tray fell *off* the table. *Not: off of* or *off from the table.*

Checkup 7. Underline the correct choices.

1. Take the cover (off, off of, off from) your typewriter and put it (behind, in back of) the books.
2. Carrie followed (in back of, behind) Ken, and Jude was (in back of, behind) Carrie.
3. The wind blew all the papers (off from, off, off of) my desk.
4. I borrowed a calculator (off of, from) Madeline.

***Over* (Not *Over With*).** *Over* says it all. *Over with* says too much!

The play is *over.* *Not: over with.*

***Until* (Not *Up Until*).** Say *until,* not *up until.*

I didn't see him *until* yesterday. *Not: up until yesterday.*

Checkup 8. Underline the correct choices.

1. We weren't sure (up until, until) we received the confirmation copy.
2. Do you think the fair is (over with, over) yet?
3. The store will be open (until, up until) 10 p.m.

***Go* and *Went* (Not *Go To* and *Went To*).** *Go to* and *went to* should not be used for *go* and *went.*

Tell me where he *went.* *Not: went to.*
Where will you *go*? *Not: go to.*

***Where* (Not *Where At*).** *Where* should not be coupled with *at.*

Find out *where* he is. *Not: is at.*

Checkup 9. Underline the correct choices.

1. Tell me where they (are at, are).
2. Did she say where they (went to, went)?
3. Where are the (scissors at, scissors)?

You can see that prepositions are very useful words. Look over the tricky ones again before you go on to conjunctions.

REVIEW QUIZ

Part 1. Underline the correct answers.

1. The fire alarm is (between, among) your office and mine.
2. Seat our guest (between, among) you and me.
3. You should (of, have) seen the mess!
4. No wonder he's angry (at, with) having to work late.
5. The job is different (from, than) my expectations.
6. Is the raise retroactive (from, to) March 15?
7. Shawn brought the paper (in to, into, in) her supervisor.
8. He was (between, among) the many candidates considered.
9. Please don't be angry (at, with) me.
10. Divide the work (between, among) all the committee members.

Part 2. Underline the correct choices.

1. Next week the seminar will be (over with, over).
2. Take the wrapper (off from, off) the package.
3. (Until, Up until) last week, I thought Mr. Gant would be our new manager.
4. Put the chair (in back of, behind) the curtain.
5. Where did he (go, go to)?
6. We scraped the paint (off of, off) the walls.
7. I need to know where the original (is, is at).
8. I wish this business were (over, over with).
9. You should wash the ink (off, off of) your hands.
10. Do you know where the books (are at, are)?

Conjunctions

Conjunctions are connectives. See the word *junction*? A junction is the place where two or more things come together, for example, the junction where roads are joined. A conjunction brings together or joins words, phrases, or clauses.

You may have noticed that not all road junctions join the same kinds of roads. Sometimes two main roads come together at a junction. At other times a small side road will hook up with the main highway. The same thing happens in sentences. There are different kinds of conjunctions; they join different kinds of sentence parts.

"EQUAL" CONJUNCTIONS

And, Or, Nor, But. *"Equal" conjunctions* are conjunctions that bring together units of equal rank or importance (equal words, equal phrases, or equal clauses). The four "equal" conjunctions are *and, or, nor,* and *but*. In the following sentences, the equal words, phrases, and clauses are in *italics*.

I had *pie* and *coffee.* The conjunction *and* joins equal words.

Does he want *to go* or *to stay*? The conjunction *or* joins equal phrases.

I did not see him,* nor *did I want to. The conjunction *nor* joins equal clauses.

We would like to help you,* but *we have no funds available. The conjunction *but* joins equal clauses.

Checkup 1. Underline the "equal" conjunctions.

1. She wrote several letters and memos this morning.
2. Do you have his phone number, or do you know his address?
3. We don't have the original contract, nor do we have a copy.
4. Their predictions are encouraging, but predictions do not always come true.
5. I do not think that the cost-of-living increase will be approved, nor do I believe that our raises will exceed 5 percent.
6. Miss Leahy recommended Anthony and Audrey for promotions.

Punctuation With "Equal" Conjunctions. Two words or two simple phrases joined by *and, but, or,* or *nor* generally require no extra punctuation.

We went to Chicago with *Gloria* and *Denise.* Two words.
She will leave *in the morning* or *in the evening.* Two phrases.

Three or more words or phrases *do* require punctuation. Note the ways commas are used with series of three or more words or phrases:

We went to Chicago with ***Gloria, Denise,*** **and** ***Margaret.*** Comma after each item except the last.

Will she leave ***in the morning, in the afternoon,*** **or** ***in the evening*****?** Comma after each item except the last.

Equal clauses, however, must be separated by commas, even if there are only two clauses.

Mrs. Barton is now on vacation, ***but*** **she will return to the office next Monday.** Comma before *but* when it joins two equal clauses.

You may purchase a copy from your newsstand, ***or*** **you may order it directly from the publisher.** Comma before *or* when it joins two equal clauses.

Remember that equal clauses are those which can stand alone. They are independent, and the comma before the conjunction stresses that the next clause is independent. To test whether clauses are independent—whether they can stand alone—read them as separate sentences without the comma and without the conjunction.

Mrs. Barton is now on vacation. She will return to the office next Monday.

You may purchase a copy from your newsstand. You may order it directly from the publisher.

As you can see, each clause is independent; each can stand alone. So, when you decide to join such clauses with the conjunctions *and, but, or,* or *nor,* be sure to place a comma before the conjunction.

Checkup 2. Underline "equal" conjunctions, and add any needed commas.

1. The volume of business will have to improve or we will have to raise prices.
2. The situation is gradually improving but we still have questions.
3. The invoices from yesterday need to be filed and today's orders need to be prepared for shipping.

Other "Equal" Conjunctions. Besides *and, but, or,* and *nor,* there are other conjunctions that can be used to join equal independent clauses. The most commonly used ones are the following:

accordingly	**besides**	**consequently**
furthermore	**hence**	**however**
likewise	**moreover**	**nevertheless**
on the contrary	**otherwise**	**then**
therefore	**thus**	**yet**
in addition		

Technically, these words are adverbs, so let's call them *adverb conjunctions.* Here is the way they are used in sentences:

We will work late today; ***furthermore,*** **we will also work late tomorrow.**

The copies are poor; ***nevertheless,*** **we must submit them.**

Checkup 3. Underline the adverb conjunctions.

1. Our work is hard; consequently, we need frequent breaks.
2. I'm not sure we can fill your order; however, we will try.
3. The shipment was late; moreover, we were short of help.

Punctuation With Adverb Conjunctions. Have you noticed a punctuation pattern for these adverb conjunctions? The examples you've seen so far look like this:

________________; however, ________________.

A semicolon usually separates the two independent clauses, the adverb conjunction follows the semicolon, and a comma follows the adverb conjunction. This is the usual way such clauses are punctuated.

Checkup 4. Punctuate the following sentences.

1. We are presenting a workshop therefore we will be out of the office.
2. The election was close consequently the votes will be recounted.
3. The new brochures will be off press next week otherwise I would already have sent you a copy.

Because the equal clauses are independent, they can stand alone as individual sentences, each ending with a period.

We will work late today. ***Furthermore,*** **we will also work late tomorrow.**
The copies are poor. ***Nevertheless,*** **we must submit them.**

Notice that the adverb conjunction is joined to the *second* clause and is followed by a comma.

Checkup 5. Separate the following clauses into two sentences. Be sure to add periods, commas, and capitals.

1. No one was prepared for the discussion therefore we didn't accomplish anything.
2. The electricity was shut off nevertheless the repairs were made.
3. The copy machine is broken in addition the cash register needs repair.

You have seen that the adverb conjunction usually is the first word in the second clause. Sometimes, however, it is placed elsewhere within the second clause.

We will work late today; we will, ***furthermore,*** **also work late tomorrow.**
The copies are poor; we must, ***nevertheless,*** **submit them.**

Now you've seen three different ways of punctuating adverb conjunctions. Let's see the distinctions:

We will work late today; ***furthermore,*** **we will also work late tomorrow.** The semicolon shows that the two clauses are closely related; therefore, the writer stresses the relationship by joining the clauses into *one* sentence.

We will work late today; we will, ***furthermore,*** **also work late tomorrow.** Again, the semicolon shows how closely related the two clauses are; the writer, however, places the adverb conjunction *furthermore* in the middle of the second clause. Note that *two* commas must set off *furthermore.*

We will work late today. ***Furthermore,*** **we will also work late tomorrow.** By using two sentences for these two ideas, the writer gives less emphasis to their close relationship. The adverb conjunction *furthermore* is sufficient to show the relationship.

Yet, Then, Thus, Hence. You have noticed that adverb conjunctions are followed by a comma. That's usual. On the other hand, a few short adverbs (*yet, then, thus,* and *hence*) are not followed by a comma. In speech, these adverbs run smoothly into the second main clause without a pause. In writing, therefore, we omit the comma, because we do not need to indicate a pause.

We tried to economize; ***yet*** **we lost money.**
We are short of paper; ***thus*** **we are sending only one copy.**

Checkup 6. Underline the adverb conjunction; then add commas where needed.

1. Miss Heinz arrived first; then the rest of the committee members arrived.
2. I must complete this report. Thus I will be here late.
3. The schedule is tight; nevertheless we will meet the deadline.
4. Your cost estimate seems accurate. You should however revise your sales estimate.
5. Our team won. Yours on the contrary lost.
6. Her goals were carefully planned; her results accordingly were impressive.

PAIRED CONJUNCTIONS

Paired conjunctions are two conjunctions always used together. There are five paired conjunctions:

Both . . . And:	**She is** ***both*** **efficient** ***and*** **knowledgeable.**
Either . . . Or:	***Either*** **you attend the first session** ***or*** **you wait until tomorrow.**
Neither . . . Nor:	**We have** ***neither*** **the time** ***nor*** **the money to complete this project.**
Not Only . . . But Also:	**The products were** ***not only*** **expensive** ***but also*** **unattractive.**
Whether . . . Or:	***Whether*** **you win** ***or*** **lose is not important.**

Checkup 7. Underline the paired conjunctions.

1. They either lost the papers or misplaced the files.
2. We can neither fill empty positions nor set up new jobs.
3. Our department head is not only progressive but also enthusiastic.
4. She has produced both radio and TV shows.
5. Do you know whether he hires part-timers or gives overtime?

Double Negatives. Be careful to avoid double negatives, that is, two negatives incorrectly used in the same sentence. Usually, double negatives involve *neither . . . nor* and the word *not* or *never.*

Wrong: **They *cannot* salvage *neither* the ship *nor* its contents.**
Cannot and _neither . . . nor_ are negatives.
Right: **They *can* salvage *neither* the ship *nor* its contents.**
Right: **They *cannot* salvage *either* the ship *or* its contents.**

As you see, you must change *neither . . . nor* to *either . . . or,* or you must change the other negative word. Let's see one more example.

Wrong: **She *never* met *neither* Mr. Higby *nor* Mrs. Poole.**
Right: **She *never* met *either* Mr. Higby *or* Mrs. Poole.**
Right: **She has met *neither* Mr. Higby *nor* Mrs. Poole.**

Checkup 8. Correct the double negatives.

1. I do not have neither the time nor the money. ____________________

____

2. The trip has never been neither fast nor pleasant. ____________________

____

3. They did not ask for neither help nor direction. ____________________

____

"UNEQUAL" CONJUNCTIONS

We've seen how "equal" conjunctions join two equal, independent clauses. The "equal" conjunctions are *and, but, or,* and *nor.* But not all clauses are independent. Some cannot stand alone. The following clauses, for example, make no sense alone because each clause gives incomplete information.

when she spoke to Mr. Hughes this morning
after Robert left the meeting
before you wrote your report
since she was promoted to manager

What happened when she spoke with Mr. Hughes? What happened after Robert left the meeting? What should you have done before you wrote your report? What happened since she was promoted to manager? These clauses are incomplete because the words *when, after, before,* and *since* lead us to expect more information. Notice that if you drop these words, the clauses would then become independent clauses.

She spoke to Mr. Hughes this morning.
Robert left the meeting.
You wrote your report.
She was promoted to manager.

You can see, then, that it is indeed the conjunction that makes each clause incomplete. The conjunctions *when, after, before,* and *since* lead us to expect more information.

How can we complete each clause? Simply by joining it to an independent clause.

When she spoke with Mr. Hughes this morning, **he asked her to send him a catalog.**

After Robert left the meeting, **he went to lunch with his boss.**

Before you wrote your report, **you should have checked the latest sales information.**

Since she was promoted to manager, **our weekly shipping volume has increased.**

Because these conjunctions are used to join two different clauses (a dependent clause + an independent clause), let's call them "unequal" conjunctions. Some of the commonly used "unequal" conjunctions are:

after	**although**	**as if**	**as though**	**because**
before	**for**	**if**	**since**	**so that**
than	**that**	**though**	**till**	**unless**
until	**when**	**where**	**whenever**	**while**

Remember that clauses starting with these words cannot stand alone as independent sentences. Note, too, that these independent clauses are not always found at the beginning of sentences, as in the above examples. They can sometimes also be placed at the end.

You should have checked the latest sales information ***before you wrote your report.***

Our weekly shipping volume has increased ***since she was promoted to manager.***

Checkup 9. Underline the "unequal" conjunctions.

1. We can't finish the assignment unless we all cooperate.
2. Mrs. Hanley received a promotion because she deserved it.
3. The advertising campaign failed, although it was expensive.
4. Whenever I leave work late, I always miss my train.

Punctuation With "Unequal" Conjunctions. Whenever a dependent clause introduces a sentence, you must use a comma after the clause. The comma slows the reader down and shows that the independent clause follows.

Although **we have a large staff, we must often hire part-timers.**

When **you call the advertising department, ask for Kim.**

The commas after *staff* and *department* tell the reader that the independent clauses follow. When the situation is reversed, the comma separating the two clauses is usually not needed:

Ask for Kim ***when*** **you call the advertising department.**

However, as you'll see later, there are some exceptions to this rule.

Checkup 10. Add commas where necessary.

1. Until she arrives we can't start the meeting.
2. Since our schedules have been changed production has increased.
3. Before I took the class I didn't know anything about finance.

TROUBLESOME CONJUNCTIONS

Watch for these troublemakers.

***Try To* (Not *Try And*).** *Try and* should not be substituted for *try to*.

She will *try to* overcome her handicap. *Not: try and overcome.*

The Reason Is That. Always say *the reason is that*, never *the reason is because*.

***The reason* I called *is that* I have had car trouble.** *Not: is because.*

Checkup 11. Underline the correct word.

1. Please try (and, to) improve your shorthand skills.
2. The reason she is leaving is (because, that) she wants to try (to, and) get a better job.
3. Miss O'Rourke said the reason for the delay is (because, that) the machine is defective.

***As, As/If, As Though* (Not *Like*).** *Like* should not be used as an "unequal" conjunction in place of *as, as if,* or *as though*. (*Like* means "similar to.")

It seems *as if* we just left. *Not: seems like.*
You sound *as though* you are in pain. *Not: like you are.*

***That* (Not *Where*).** *Where* should not be used in place of *that* in sentences such as:

I read in the paper *that* crime is decreasing. *Not: where crime.*

Checkup 12. Underline the correct word.

1. It looks (like, as if) we have met the deadline.
2. I suppose you saw the announcement (where, that) Jack is retiring.
3. Did you read in the paper (where, that) the mayor is talking (as though, like) her reelection were a sure thing?

***So That* (Not *So*).** *So* should not be used with a dependent clause that shows purpose or intent. Instead, use *so that.*

Bring your family *so that* we can meet them. *Not: so we can.*

To check whether your sentence shows purpose or intent, ask yourself "Why?"

Bring your family. Why? *So that* we can meet them.
Take your time. Why? *So that* you will do a good job.

Checkup 13. Underline the correct conjunction.

1. I bought a car (so, so that) I could travel to Iowa this summer.
2. They installed a postage meter (so, so that) we could handle our own mail.
3. The conference room was opened (so, so that) everyone could attend.
4. It certainly appears (like, as though) the merger will be approved.

REVIEW QUIZ

Part 1. Underline errors in conjunction usage, and write your correction in the space provided. Write *OK* if a sentence is correct.

1. It has neither style or price advantage. 1. ________
2. We don't know neither the supervisor or the manager. 2. ________
3. You may give this copy to John or Brett. 3. ________
4. He said he had neither time nor money to write. 4. ________
5. Not only Miss Dix also Mr. Hert went to the workshop. 5. ________
6. Both the accounting department or the advertising department are on this floor. 6. ________
7. We have never had a convention in Miami nor Dallas. 7. ________
8. How can you tell whether this is correct nor not? 8. ________
9. The folder was neither in the file or on her desk. 9. ________
10. She said she had not met neither of the owners. 10. ________

Part 2. Underline errors in conjunction usage or in punctuation. Write your correction in the space provided. Write *OK* if a sentence is correct.

1. Did you read in the company paper where a profit-sharing plan will soon be announced? 1. ________
2. Please send your application so we can make an evaluation. 2. ________
3. Sam planned to go to the meeting however he had to change his plans. 3. ________
4. We asked the supervisor to try and dictate more slowly. 4. ________
5. The reason for his happiness is because he is being promoted. 5. ________
6. Jim reacted like he had been blamed for the error. 6. ________
7. We read in the paper where the mayor was resigning. 7. ________
8. The stock market soared nevertheless we continued to lose business. 8. ________
9. He said the reason for the change was because a new law had been passed. 9. ________
10. Although his work load is heavy Erin enjoys the challenge. 10 ________

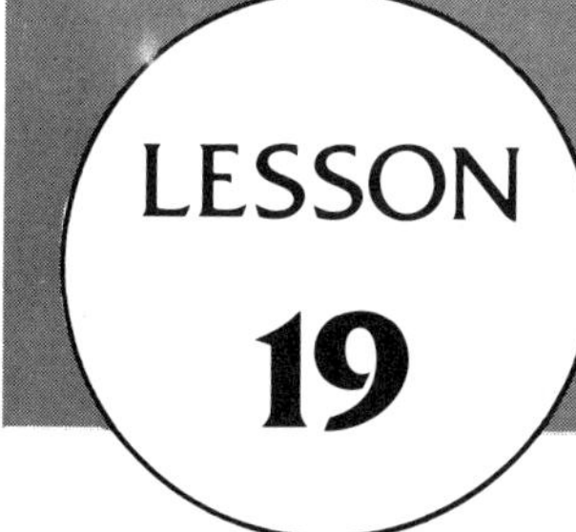

SECTION 5 WRAP-UP:

Modifiers and Connectives

The next few pages will bring together the ideas you've learned about adjectives, adverbs, prepositions, and conjunctions. Remember that adjectives and adverbs make your message colorful and specific by giving extra information. Prepositions and conjunctions then connect the different units so that your messages hang together.

Look over the reminders and review the section material before completing the Spelling Exercise.

The following statements are reminders of common, irritating mistakes found in everyday business correspondence. Do your best to avoid them!

Errors: **She is the neat*est* of the two.**
Pick the *best* of the two.

When comparing two items, use the comparative, not the superlative, form of the adjective.

Corrections: **She is the neat*er* of the two.**
Pick the bett*er* of the two.

Error: **Our brand has *less* calories.**

Fewer is used with plural nouns to tell *how many. Less* is used with singular nouns to tell *how much*.

Correction: **Our brand has *fewer* calories, and it costs *less* money.**

Error: **These directions are *real* clear.**

Real is an adjective; *really* is an adverb. Adjectives modify only nouns. In the sentence above, *clear* is an adjective modifying *directions.* Only an adverb can modify the adjective *clear;* thus *really* is correct.

Correction: **These directions are *really* clear.**

Error: **I feel *badly* about your loss.**

Don't ever say "I feel *badly.*" The linking verb *feel* requires the adjective *bad* to describe the subject *I.*

Correction: **I feel *bad* about your loss.**

Error: **Divide the cost *between* the four of us.**

Between refers to two items; *among* refers to three or more items.

Correction: **Divide the cost *among* the four of us.**

Error: **The reason I am late is *because* I was snowed in.**

Whenever you see "the reason is," make sure *that,* not *because,* follows.

Correction: **The reason I am late is *that* I was snowed in.**

Now go on to the Spelling Exercise. Before you do, review the rules about forming adverbs. Use your dictionary as often as necessary.

SPELLING EXERCISE

Correct all the misspelled adjectives. Place a *C* after an adjective that is correctly spelled. Then write the adverb form in the Adverb column, as in the example. Be ready for a spelling quiz.

		CORRECT SPELLING	ADVERB
0.	emphatic	C	emphatically
1.	accessable		
2.	mechanicle		
3.	possibal		
4.	permisible		
5.	circumstantal		
6.	negligible		
7.	mischievous		
8.	preferrable		
9.	curteus		
10.	derrogatory		
11.	desireable		
12.	embarassing		
13.	illigitimute		
14.	seperate		
15.	excelent		

Internal Punctuation Marks

YOUR GOALS

After finishing this section, you will be able to:

1. Correctly use commas with:
   a. Items in a series.
   b. Adjectives.
   c. Introductory expressions.
   d. Words in direct address.
   e. Restatements.
   f. Abbreviated titles.
   g. City, state, and country names.
   h. Dates.
   i. Numbers.
   j. Contrasting statements.
   k. Direct quotations.
2. Recognize and correctly punctuate:
   a. Simple sentences.
   b. Compound sentences.
   c. Complex sentences.
   d. Compound-complex sentences.
3. Correctly use semicolons to join independent clauses and to separate complex items in a series.
4. Correctly use colons:
   a. With expressions of time.
   b. In ratios.
   c. After salutations.
   d. Following introductory words.
   e. Before explanatory sentences and rules.
   f. Before lists.
   g. Before lengthy quotations.
5. Correctly use periods in decimals and abbreviations and in ellipses to show omitted words.
6. Use question marks and exclamation points correctly.
7. Correctly spell 15 frequently misspelled words, using them in sentences that include commas, semicolons, and colons.

Commas

COMMAS—GENERAL USE

A comma is like the highway sign that says *slow.* It signals a slight pause or an interruption. Since you will use this mark very often, you must know its different uses.

Items in a Series. Three or more equal items (single words, sets of phrases, or independent clauses) should be separated by commas. Note that a comma is used after each item *except* the last.

Series of Adjectives Before a Noun:	**The** *first, second,* **and** *third* **answers are correct.**
Series of Adjectives Following a Linking Verb:	**The flag is** *red, white,* **and** *blue.*
Series of Verb Phrases:	**We came here** *to hike, to swim,* **and** *to relax.*
	Karen *contacted the committee, reserved a conference room, sent out notices,* **and** *chaired the meeting.*
Series of Clauses:	*Angie gathered the information, Jeff prepared an outline,* **and** *Harvey wrote the report.*

Notice that within a series all items are *equal.*

first = second = third   **to hike = to swim = to relax**

Angie gathered the information = Jeff prepared an outline = Harvey wrote the report

This relationship of units is called *parallelism.* Later we'll talk more about parallelism and equality of items in a series.

Checkup 1. Add commas to separate items in a series.

1. The yellow the blue and the pink copies are distributed to branch offices.
2. I went because the location was convenient the time was appropriate and the speaker was famous.
3. He will have to gather the information organize the facts type the report and present the evidence.

Use of *Etc.* The abbreviation *etc.* means "and so forth." Notice that *etc.* ends with a period. When *etc.* is part of a series within a sentence, you need a comma both before and after the abbreviation. Of course, do not use two periods when *etc.* ends a sentence. Never say "and etc." This would actually mean "and and so forth."

We packed food, clothing, equipment, ***etc.,*** **for our trip.**

COMMA BEFORE AND AFTER

We camped, swam, fished, ***etc.***

ONLY ONE PERIOD

Checkup 2. Add commas and periods where needed.

1. Steak chicken spaghetti etc were on the menu.
2. They manufacture cards games novelties etc
3. There are dishes food etc in the cupboard.

Commas With Adjectives. You've already seen commas used to separate adjectives.

He bought a ***sleek, expensive*** **car.**
She sold her ***long, black, soft*** **mink.**

These are "equal" adjectives in the sense that each modifies the same noun. *Sleek* and *expensive* both modify *car. Long, black,* and *soft* all modify *mink.* Therefore, each adjective is followed by a comma except the last adjective—the one immediately before the noun. There is no comma after the last adjective, of course!

Checkup 3. Add commas where needed.

1. They sent us a long complicated survey.
2. Gloria wrote a clear interesting proposal.
3. She suggested a practical inexpensive solution.

Beware of two-word nouns. They may tempt you to place commas incorrectly.

Where is the weekly *payroll report*? *Weekly* modifies the two-word noun *payroll report*. No comma after *weekly*.
He bought a sleek, expensive *sports car*. The noun is *sports car*. No comma after *expensive*.

One other situation requires your attention. Usually do not use commas to separate adjectives in sentences such as these:

Mrs. Hague bought an *old brown* house.
↑
NO COMMA

I placed a *small red* bow on the packages.
↑
NO COMMA

Although *brown house* is not a two-word noun, we still consider *old* as modifying the idea "brown house." Likewise, we consider *small* as modifying the idea "red bow." If you wouldn't say "old *and* brown house" or "small *and* red bow," don't use a comma to separate the adjectives.

Many adjectives referring to size, age, and number often are written without commas after them. Remember to use *and* to test whether a comma is needed.

He needs *two good* helpers.
↑
NO COMMA

She hired *four teenage* part-timers for the summer.
↑
NO COMMA

Checkup 4. Add commas where needed.

1. Three important yellow pages were missing from the price list.
2. Our two new secretaries write clear concise letters.
3. She donated her old wood desk to charity.

Commas After Introductory Expressions. Introductory words, phrases, or clauses are usually set off by commas. Each of these expressions introduces—leads up to—the main thought in the sentence. The introductory expressions in the following sentences are in *italics*.

Introductory Word:	*Fortunately,* **the door was open.**
Prepositional Phrase:	*With your talent and my energy,* **we could surely succeed.**
Verb Phrase:	*To achieve success,* **you also need luck.**
Phrase With Present Participle:	*Reaching the top of the ladder,* **he climbed onto the roof.**
Introductory Clause:	*If you need help,* **give me a call.**

Once again, our preference for neat, uncluttered correspondence gives us a bit of freedom. When a sentence begins with a very short prepositional phrase, we can do without the usual comma, *unless* the message might be misunderstood without the comma.

In the house **I have several technical dictionaries.**
↑
NO COMMA NEEDED

At noon **we usually go out for lunch.**
↑
NO COMMA NEEDED

But: ***In 1963,*** **421 members paid dues.**
↑
COMMA NEEDED FOR CLARITY

Checkup 5. Add commas where needed.

1. After the last show of the series he will retire.
2. In the morning we'll leave for Hawaii.
3. Hurrying to the elevator she stumbled and fell.
4. To succeed in this business you need to be alert.
5. When the plane arrives we will be waiting.
6. As soon as the check is signed mail it to Mrs. Perez.

Direct Address. Words in direct address are set off by commas. The words in direct address are the name of the person addressed or a substitute for his or her name.

I am not sure, ***miss,*** **whether that calculator is in stock.**
I think, ***sir,*** **you may be eligible for a discount.**
You suggested, ***Mrs. Ramsey,*** **that we hire a consultant.**
Yes, ***Doctor,*** **I will check the report immediately.**

Of course, if the words in direct address begin the sentence, then only one comma is used—following the words in direct address. Notice that the words *miss* and *sir* begin with small letters if they are not followed by a proper name, while other proper names or titles used in direct address are capitalized.

Restatements. Restatements following a noun are set off by commas. Restatements are repetitions of a noun in different words.

Mrs. Freeport, ***president of our branch,*** **has approved the loan.**
His most famous book, ***My Life in Congress,*** **is on the best-seller list.**

President of our branch is another way of saying what? *My Life in Congress* is another way of saying what?

Checkup 6. Add commas where needed.

1. Miss Clark the receptionist will make an appointment for you.
2. I hope sir that you receive your shipment by Monday.
3. Miss Rand please allow us to replace the damaged items.
4. As you know Charles the new word processing equipment will be delivered this week.
5. Please bill all the duplicating costs to my supervisor Janet Slocum.
6. The defendant Ted Trump refused to discuss the trial with reporters.

Abbreviated Titles. Abbreviations of certain terms following a person's or a company's name are generally set off by two commas. Note, for example, how *Jr.*, *M.D.*, and *Inc.* are set off.

Henry P. Silver, *Jr.,* has inherited the business.
Caroline Bergstrom, *M.D.,* addressed the group.
Randall and Bruske, *Inc.,* went bankrupt last year.

However, writers always follow a preference indicated by a person or a company. For example, *Time Inc.* uses no comma in its name.

We sent the check to Time *Inc.* last Friday.

Henry P. Silver *Jr.* has inherited the business. Correct if Mr. Silver writes his name without a comma before *Jr.*

Also, drop the second comma when such abbreviations must be made possessive.

Randall and Bruske, *Inc.'s* headquarters was formerly located in Canton, Ohio.

Roman Numerals. Roman numerals following a name are not set off by commas.

Fred Manor *III* owns most of the stock.
↑ ↑
NO COMMAS

Checkup 7. Add commas where needed. Write *OK* after the sentence if no commas are needed.

1. The reign of King Henry II was the subject of her doctoral thesis.
2. Fred Reed Jr.'s home is magnificent.
3. Faber and Faber Inc. predicted the merger.
4. Evelyn J. Bartelli Ph.D. is the vice president in charge of our Canadian office.

City, State, and Country Names. State and country names that follow a city name are set off from the rest of the sentence by commas, *both* before and after.

COMMA COMMA
↓ ↓
***Minneapolis, Minnesota,* is my home.**

From *Montreal, Canada,* we traveled to *Boston, Massachusetts,* and finally to *Stockholm, Sweden.*

However, no comma separates the ZIP Code from the rest of the address.

Send it to Merton, Minnesota *56123,* as soon as possible.
Not: *Minnesota, 56123.*

Checkup 8. Add commas where needed.

1. Fairchild Iowa was the site we selected.
2. The strike at our Kingsley Florida plant was unexpected.
3. One of the packages addressed to Lake Miles Arizona 73102 was lost.

Dates. You've often seen that two commas are used to set off the year in month/day/year dates.

On *April 12, 1980,* my sister was elected senior partner in her law firm.

Write month/year dates *without* commas. (It isn't wrong to include commas; it's just unnecessary.)

My boss is scheduled to retire in *May 1986.*

Checkup 9. Add commas where needed. Write *OK* after the sentence if no commas are needed.

1. Please send me a copy of the February 3 1978 issue of *Business Week.*
2. The next time our convention will be held in New York City will be in October 1984 or in November 1985.
3. I last saw Miss Dandridge at a seminar on March 12 1980.

Numbers. Commas are used to separate numbers into groups of threes.

Her fee was only $4,750.
We drove 17,000 miles last year.
The company was sold for $12,450,000 (according to the *Wall Street Journal*).

The following groups of numbers are exceptions! These *don't* require commas.

Phone Number:	**555 612-6121**	*Page Number:*	**page 1361**
House Number:	**13251 Bright Avenue**	*ZIP Code:*	**55991**
Serial Number:	**No. 63841**	*Decimal:*	**0.4382**

Checkup 10. Add commas where needed.

1. The overhead cost is $10950 a year.
2. Check page 2016 for information on the 1000-mile warranty.
3. Of last year's 480000 orders, only 1100 were shipped out of state.

Contrasting Statements. Commas are used to set off opposing or contrasting statements that interrupt the flow of the sentence. These statements begin with such words as *not, rather, but,* and *though.*

OPPOSITE

It's action, not words, we need now.

NORMAL FLOW OF SENTENCE

CONTRAST

We asked Peter, rather than Mark, to check the statistics.

NORMAL FLOW OF SENTENCE

CONTRAST

We caught the earliest, though not the fastest, train home.

NORMAL FLOW OF SENTENCE

Checkup 11. Draw a box around opposing or contrasting statements, and add commas where needed.

1. It was you not Harold whom they wanted.
2. The firm selected Texas rather than Missouri for its branch office.
3. This is the brightest though not the neatest room.
4. He was the first but not the only applicant for the job.

Direct Quotations. Direct quotations (a person's exact words) are set off with commas.

He said, "We will be pleased to see you."
I replied, "If you stay away too long, we may forget you."

Checkup 12. Add commas where needed.

1. Mrs. Matos said "This is an excellent suggestion, Mark."
2. "That's too much" I replied.
3. He said "Let me know if you need me."

The comma can certainly be used in a lot of ways, can't it? Review the uses we've covered so far. Can you use the comma correctly in a series? with *etc.*? with adjectives? after introductory expressions? in direct address? with restatements? with abbreviated titles? with names of states and countries? in dates? with numbers? with opposing or contrasting statements? with direct quotations? You should be able to!

REVIEW QUIZ

Add commas where needed. Remove any unnecessary commas.

1. Elaine O. Berg Ph.D. opened her office in Callender Nevada.
2. It will be Shirley not Pat who will do the driving.
3. They lived in Columbus Ohio and Chicago Illinois before coming to Dubuque Iowa.
4. January, 1977, broke several temperature records in International City Wisconsin and Huron Indiana.
5. We agree Ms. Tooke that the invoice is incorrect.
6. At 2:30 11 students will receive their diplomas.
7. Newspapers magazines etc. will be collected for recycling.
8. Travel fine clothes expensive jewelry and fame will be yours.
9. The zoo had monkeys bears lions tigers etc.
10. The muddy crooked road led to a tiny white house.

11. Our office used to be Calvin Ohio, 34,567. However we have since moved.

12. Mrs. French saw the accident rescued the victim and called an ambulance.

13. On February 10 1974 the price of this stock was the highest of more than 2000 stocks listed.

14. Could we invite Stan Warner, II, to be our speaker?

15. After reviewing the figures Phoebe our accountant said "I have found a serious error."

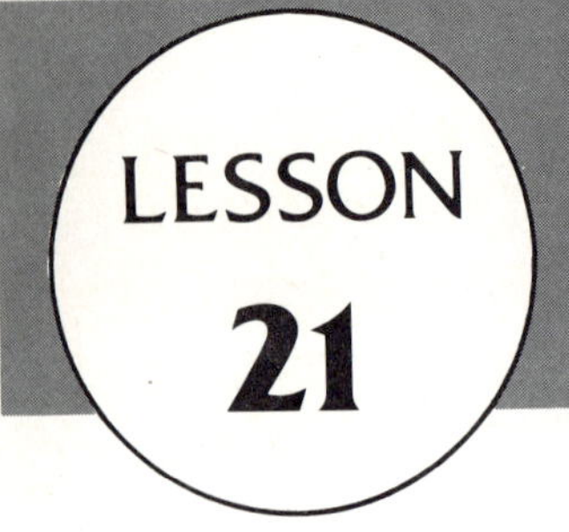

LESSON 21 Commas With Clauses

A BRIEF REVIEW

We've seen that commas are useful to set apart all kinds of miscellaneous units within a sentence. Before we review the uses of the comma, let's define some of these units to be sure you will be able to recognize them.

Phrases and Clauses. We've talked several times about *phrases* and *clauses.* In what way are they different?

A *phrase* is a group of two or more words that contains only a subject or a verb.

Examples: **to the convention** **near my office**

A *clause* is a group of words containing both a subject and a verb.

Examples: ***Kay went*** **to the convention.**
While *she was checking* the figures . . .

Next, what's the difference between an independent clause and a dependent clause?

An *independent clause* contains a complete thought and can stand alone as a sentence.

Examples: **Kay went to the convention.**
She was checking the figures.

As you see, each of the above expresses a complete thought. Therefore, each can stand alone as a sentence. They are *independent clauses.*

A *dependent clause* does not contain a complete thought and cannot stand alone. It is tied to the main thought in the sentence by an "unequal" conjunction.

Examples: ***When*** **Kay went to the fair . . .**
While **she was checking the figures . . .**

Notice that the "unequal" conjunctions lead us to expect more information to complete the thought.

Checkup 1. In the space provided, write an *I* for each independent clause and a *D* for each dependent clause.

1. Because we had nothing else to do. 1. ______
2. Few people know the principles of time management. 2. ______
3. Until we have a better opportunity. 3. ______
4. As soon as we receive the invoice. 4. ______

Now let's review some of the uses of the comma.

Commas for Clarity. First, let's look at the following sentence.

When we turn off the TV lamps on the end tables light the room.

Confusing, isn't it? Now let's use a comma to show where the pause belongs.

When we turn off the TV, lamps on the end tables light the room.

We talked about using *when, if, since,* and other adverb conjunctions, remember? *When* and other adverb conjunctions introduce *clauses. When* is one of the "unequal" conjunctions that signal a dependent clause, and we need the comma to show a pause between this dependent clause and the independent clause that follows.

Checkup 2. Add commas to separate dependent clauses from main clauses.

1. Because it is December we can expect snow any day.
2. If you want to lose weight you must eat less and exercise more.
3. Until we hire another staff member we will be very busy.
4. After Robyn leaves for San Antonio we will start working on the Anderson project.

Comma Before "Equal" Conjunctions. Another case we discussed in our lesson on conjunctions was the use of a comma before an "equal" conjunction: *and, or, nor,* or *but.* You saw that these conjunctions join equal independent clauses. Remember the test for independent clauses? Each part could stand alone as a separate sentence if you removed the "equal" conjunction. When the parts are joined, the comma signals a pause between two major, equal units.

Joined: **Owning my own business was enjoyable, *but* I had to work very long hours.**

Separate: **Owning my own business was enjoyable. *But* I had to work very long hours.**

Checkup 3. Add commas between independent clauses.

1. All of us learned how to sort files but only two of us learned how to store them.
2. The company offered a contract and the union agreed to the proposal.
3. We have to reorder supplies or we will run short for the conference.
4. We have no complaints nor do we expect to have any.

Comma With "Equal" Adverbs. Except for *yet, then, thus,* and *hence,* "equal" adverbs are set off by commas.

My time is up; *nevertheless,* I am not finished.
Time is short. We will, *however,* meet the deadline.

Checkup 4. Add commas to set off "equal" adverbs.

1. Jerry comes to work early. Sean however usually comes late.
2. My office has a carpeted floor. Moreover it has a window.
3. She is very efficient. Therefore she is likely to be promoted.
4. Mrs. Fasano has excellent management potential. Consequently she has been asked to attend a special executive-training program.

DEPENDENT CLAUSE FOLLOWING INDEPENDENT CLAUSE

We've seen that a dependent clause that comes *before* the main clause is followed by a comma. The comma signals a pause before heading into the main idea. How about sentences with the dependent clause coming *after* the main clause? Are they also separated from the main clause by a comma? Well, that depends. You first have to decide whether the information in the dependent clause is *essential*—really necessary—to the main thought of the sentence.

Nonessential Information. If the additional information in the dependent clause is not really necessary to the main thought of the sentence, it should be set off by commas.

We will call you early next week, ***when we have more information.***

The statement *early next week* already establishes the time; the *when* clause simply provides extra but unnecessary information about "next week." Therefore, a comma is needed.

Here's another example.

Jim, ***who will be working with you,*** **will arrive tonight.**

The *who* clause simply presents additional information about Jim. It's interesting to know that Jim will be working with you, but the main message in this sentence is, "Jim will arrive tonight." Since the additional information isn't really necessary, the clause should be set off by commas.

Checkup 5. Add commas to set off nonessential clauses.

1. The rent was raised although the taxes had gone down.
2. We went to Columbus where the convention was held.
3. The new file clerk who is a friend of mine will start next week.

Essential Information. Now let's look at a couple of sentences with an essential dependent clause. These sentences may look something like our examples of nonessential information, but they're not the same.

We will call you ***when we have more information.***

In this sentence the *when* clause gives essential information. It tells specifically when "we will call you." Therefore, no comma separates this essential dependent clause from the main clause. It all flows together.

Here's another example. Compare it to our second example of nonessential information.

Jim is the writer ***who will be working with you.***

In this sentence we need the *who* clause to identify Jim and to complete the meaning of the sentence. Thus we don't separate these two clauses with a comma. Do you see the difference?

Checkup 6. Add commas where needed. Don't set off essential clauses. Write *C* if the sentence is correct without commas.

1.	We began to wonder if he was coming.	1. ______
2.	We expect you to notify us when the payment is due.	2. ______
3.	I should finish this work since I'll be gone tomorrow.	3. ______

"Unequal" Conjunctions Requiring a Comma. The following list will be helpful in deciding whether a clause contains essential information or not. These unequal conjunctions *always* lead into nonessential clauses, which are correctly set off by commas.

although	**none of which**	**none of whom**	**all of which**	**which**
though	**some of which**	**some of whom**	**all of whom**	**whereas**

In the following sentences, the nonessential information is in *italics*.

The four-day work week went into effect, ***although it was not a popular idea.***
All staff members, ***some of whom are new,*** **received large raises.**

Checkup 7. Add commas where needed.

1. They submitted three proposals none of which were acceptable.
2. She did not win the tournament although she was leading yesterday.
3. Our group has signed the contract whereas your group has not settled.

KINDS OF SENTENCES

The simplest kind of sentence has only one clause. More complicated sentences may contain three or more clauses, depending on how you want to tie your thoughts together. Where you put commas will depend on how you put the pieces together.

Simple Sentence. A sentence containing just one thought is called—logically—a *simple sentence.* There are no dependent clauses tacked on.

SUBJECT VERB
The telephone rang three times.

SUBJECT VERB
I ordered a hamburger.

DOUBLE SUBJECT DOUBLE VERB
Marge and Rosa came into the office and left their reports.

Remember: Having a double subject and/or a double verb doesn't make two clauses! In this clause two subjects *share* two verbs in *one* main thought.

Since a simple sentence has only one clause, there are no dependent clauses to set off with commas. That doesn't mean, however, that simple sentences never have commas. It just means that any commas in a simple sentence are needed for some other reason (for example, to separate "equal" adjectives, to set off words in direct address or contrasting statements, or to separate items in series).

Checkup 8. Underline the subject once and the verb twice in these simple sentences.

1. Smoke filled the stuffy, crowded room.
2. The Madison Hotel opened yesterday.
3. Karen went home, not to work.

Compound Sentences. When you join two independent clauses with an "equal" conjunction (*and, or, nor,* or *but*), you have a *compound sentence.* Just as a compound subject contains more than one subject, and a compound verb contains more than one verb, a compound sentence contains more than one sentence. You've already learned that a comma goes before the "equal" conjunction, but here's one more example.

The papers will be ready Tuesday, and we will sign them on Wednesday.

↑ COMMA SEPARATES TWO INDEPENDENT CLAUSES

Checkup 9. Add commas in these compound sentences.

1. The book was completed on schedule but publishing was delayed.
2. They will take the bus or they will come by train.
3. Ann was transferred to Arizona and Terri moved to Montreal.
4. Mrs. Perkins developed all these policies and procedures and she expects us to follow them closely.

Complex Sentences. When you tie together one main clause and one or more dependent clauses, you get a *complex sentence.* You've been working with complex sentences all along, so they're nothing new. You also know that the dependent clauses can come either before or after the independent clause. They may or may not need a comma. Now let's look at more examples of complex sentences.

COMMA NEEDED ↓

When we set up our word processing center, our efficiency increased 20 percent. (Dependent Clause + Independent Clause)

They changed the policy because we objected when they raised prices. (Independent Clause + Two Dependent Clauses: *because we objected* and *when they raised prices*)

Checkup 10. Add commas to these complex sentences.

1. Because we were on strike the billing was late last month.
2. Since we are all here let's start the meeting.
3. We'll leave on time although we have a lot to do.
4. Whenever Ms. Daly and her assistant come to the East Coast on business they always stay a few extra days.

Compound-Complex Sentences. What happens when you join two independent clauses with at least one dependent clause? Of course! You get a compound-complex sentence.

Independent Clause: **The president of the union made a speech,**
↖ COMMA NEEDED

\+

Independent Clause: **and the workers formed picket lines,**
↑ EQUAL CONJUNCTION ↖ COMMA NEEDED

\+

Dependent Clause: **although their demands had already been met.**
↑ UNEQUAL CONJUNCTION

To punctuate a compound-complex sentence, follow this procedure:

1. Separate the two independent clauses by placing a comma before the "equal" conjunction.
2. Punctuate each half as a separate sentence.
3. Add a comma between the dependent and independent clause—if a comma is needed.

Here's a different example of a compound-complex sentence:

Dependent Clause: **When working conditions are poor,**
UNEQUAL CONJUNCTION COMMA NEEDED

\+

Independent Clause: **employees are unhappy with their jobs,**
OPTIONAL COMMA

\+

Independent Clause: **and production generally decreases.**
EQUAL CONJUNCTION

Checkup 11. Add commas to these compound-complex sentences.

1. When she comes to visit we will meet her at the airport and we will take her to her hotel.
2. Salaries have gone up but taxes have also risen although we have a new administrator.
3. Since it is our rush season we must hire more help or we will have to work overtime.

That's all you need to know about commas to separate clauses. None of it is hard *if* you remember to look at each clause to see what it's joined to. Draw diagrams, if necessary, to get a picture of the parts of the sentence.

REVIEW QUIZ

Add commas where needed.

1. Since you're my friend will you help me with this?
2. You know however that we're changing our plans.
3. The mail none of which was ours arrived at 9 a.m. and a large package was delivered an hour later.
4. When the conference dates have been set we will get in touch with you and we will plan our strategy.
5. Until my secretary joins us I will take notes.
6. The sorting was not completed nor was the mail delivered.
7. The office equipment was sold and all the records were transferred to Ike's department where they will be available for the accountants.

8. I don't know if he plans to leave for Detroit tomorrow.
9. The messenger managed to keep the car on the road although a tire blew out when he hit a sharp rock.
10. We'll all be able to go to the luncheon unless an emergency occurs before tomorrow.
11. Shall we plan the party for December when everyone will be in a festive mood?
12. I'll be ready whenever you are.
13. The bus that goes to Markton comes from Crowley where the bus company has its main terminal.
14. The office manager and the plant supervisor had a meeting and they resolved all the problems quickly and satisfactorily.
15. Because these statistics are so important we need to spend some time studying them.

Other Punctuation Marks

SEMICOLON

Notice how the semicolon is constructed; it combines a comma and a period. The semicolon is a mark of separation that's stronger than a comma but weaker than a period.

Semicolon Joining Independent Clauses. The most common use of a semicolon is to join two closely related independent clauses that aren't linked by an "equal" conjunction.

Our Minnesota branch placed first in the sales contest; our Wisconsin branch, for some reason, came in last.

Often the second clause will begin with a transitional word or phrase, such as an "equal" adverb.

I was offered the promotion; *nevertheless,* I resigned to accept another position.

Checkup 1. Add semicolons where needed.

1. My son won a scholarship therefore, we moved to Ohio.
2. They made an offer we accepted their bid.
3. The girls are coming today moreover, they are staying for the weekend.

Two independent clauses joined by a semicolon also could be written as two separate sentences. Look at how the sentences on page 141 can be rewritten without semicolons.

Our Minnesota branch placed first in the sales contest. Our Wisconsin branch, for some reason, came in last.

I was offered the promotion. Nevertheless, I resigned to accept another position.

Checkup 2. Rewrite as separate sentences.

1. Todd works in the accounting department; his twin brother Tim is in law school. ______________________________

   ____

2. Six inches of snow fell; nevertheless, we held our conference. ______________________________

   ____

3. The comma is the most used punctuation mark; it is also the most overused mark. ______________________________

   ____

4. Give this invoice to Jeffrey or Inez for approval; if neither one is available, then give it to Mrs. Dubron. ______________________________

   ____

Semicolon in a Series. The semicolon also may be used instead of a comma to separate items in a series when a comma occurs in one or more of the items.

The committee was made up of Howard Delaney, Amoritin Corporation, Memphis, Tennessee; Silas Brown, Darton's, Inc., Atlantic City, New Jersey; and Mabel Karley, Reuther's, Miami, Florida.

With commas in place of these semicolons, there would be 12 commas in this sentence. It would be hard to tell where one item ended and the next began.

Checkup 3. Add semicolons where needed.

We ordered 20 vases, No. 6F234, page 232, 16 bulbs, No. 5B462, page 116, 12 decorations, No. 2D4326, page 98, and 24 tapes, No. 4T3861, page 246.

COLONS

Colons usually mean that something closely related will follow.

Colons With Time, Ratios, and Salutations. You've already used colons in expressions of time, in ratios, and in salutations of letters:

6:15 p.m. **a 3:1 sand-concrete mix** (Read: a three-to-one . . .)
Dear Mr. Reaney:

Colons With Emphatic Introductory Words. To catch a reader's attention, an emphatic statement often is introduced by a single word followed by a colon.

Note: Read this section carefully. **Remember: You must check out by 6 p.m.**

Notice that full sentences following an emphatic introductory word begin with a capital letter.

Colons With Explanatory Sentences and Formal Rules. Sometimes an introductory sentence will lead into a second sentence that gives an example or an explanation. The lead-in sentence often uses such summarizing words as *this is, these,* or *the following.* Such introductory sentences are separated from the example or explanation by a colon, and the second sentence is capitalized.

This is the rule to apply: Declarative sentences end with periods.
His reasons for moving include the following: He sold his business, his family is grown, and his health is failing.

Checkup 4. Add colons and capital letters where needed. (***Remember:*** To capitalize a lowercase letter, underscore the letter three times.)

1. We stand a 4 1 chance of making the 7 20 train.
2. Attention the office will close at 2 30 p.m. on December 24.
3. This is all I have to say keep up the good work!

Colons With Lists. Often a series of words or phrases will follow an independent clause in the middle of a sentence, without being set off from the rest of the paragraph. The independent clause usually includes summarizing words such as *these* or *the following*.

We are looking for these qualities: intelligence, ambition, efficiency, and loyalty.

Note that the first word following the colon is not capitalized. Note, too, that a complete sentence *precedes* the colon.

We are looking for:	**We are looking for these qualities:**
Intelligence.	**1. Intelligence**
Ambition.	**2. Ambition**
Efficiency.	**3. Efficiency**
Loyalty.	**4. Loyalty**

The numbers are optional. They provide extra emphasis and an easy way for the reader to refer to the items. Do you see that the items in one list end in periods, but the items in the other list do not? The reason is simply that in the first list, each item *completes* the introductory statement *We are looking for . . . .* In the second, the introductory statement *We are looking for these qualities* is already complete. Because the items that follow do not complete the second statement, no periods are needed. One last thing: Note that each item in both lists begins with a capital letter.

Let's look at one more example:

The union demanded:

1. **Higher wages for clerical workers.**
2. **Shorter hours for the professional staff.**
3. **Increased medical benefits for all employees.**

Do you understand why each item ends in a period? Now look at this sentence when it is not in "list" form:

The union demanded higher wages for clerical workers, shorter hours for the professional staff, and increased medical benefits for all employees.

As you see, no colon is needed after *demanded,* because it does not introduce a tabulated list. A colon here would only interrupt the sentence, as it does in the following example:

Wrong: **Some of the specialties included: Italian, French, and German favorites.**

Right: **Some of the specialties included Italian, French, and German favorites.**

The colon interrupts the sentence in such cases. However, note how the words *the following* change the sentence:

Some of the specialties included the following: Italian, French, and German favorites.

Here, the colon introduces a list without interrupting the complete sentence.

Checkup 5. Add colons, periods, and capitals where needed.

1. For the picnic we purchased these items pretzels, potato chips, and salted peanuts.
2. Next November we'll vote for a mayor, a senator, and a governor.
3. The positions we have open are
    1. clerk typist
    2. account clerk
    3. clerk stenographer

Colons Before Quotations. Before a long, formal quotation, a colon may be used instead of a comma.

The board of directors responded this way: "The proposal you submitted is interesting, and it may prove to be useful in the future; however, the company cannot, at this time, risk further funds. If you wish to contact us later this year, we may be able to reconsider."

Note that the quotation must be introduced by an independent clause.

Checkup 6. Add colons where needed.

1. This is the way his speech started "You can't imagine how glad I am to be here today. This is a privilege I've dreamed about for years. Thank you for inviting me."
2. Mrs. West had this to say "I have received your manuscript and will review it as soon as possible. Comments will be forwarded for your consideration in making revisions. Keep up the good work!"

PERIODS

Periods in Numbers and Abbreviations. Periods are used in decimal and dollar numbers and in many abbreviations:

0.6 gram	**13.12 percent**	**66.30 k/h**	**$123.56**
Mrs.	**Mr.**	**Dr.**	**Ph.D.**
c.o.d.	**f.o.b.**	**Co.**	**Ltd.**
St.	**U.S.**	**max.**	**R.S.V.P.**

However, there also are many abbreviations that do *not* use periods, among them all the two-letter state abbreviations and all abbreviations of units of measure (both metric and customary).

MN	**NY**	**WI**	**NH**
MT	**KY**	**TX**	**AL**
gal	**pt**	**qt**	**oz**
g	**l**	**m**	**cm**

Use an authoritative reference manual whenever you need to check abbreviations. And be sure *not* to double the period when an abbreviation with a period ends a sentence:

Thomas Jacobs, Sr., is the comptroller for Marks, Inc. *Not:* *Marks, Inc..*

Checkup 7. Add periods where needed.

1. The swatches measure 0 3 in x 001 in
2. Does Ms Dulles still live in Rochester, MN?
3. They brought food, dishes, games, prizes, etc

Ellipses. A series of three periods is called an *ellipsis* (plural: *ellipses*). An ellipsis may be used to show that some of the words in a quotation have been left out. Compare the following full quotation with the shortened version using an ellipsis.

Full Quotation: **Ms. Katz, our director of sales, replied, "To increase our share of the home-appliance market, we must develop strategies that will make our products more competitive and more attractive to potential buyers."**

Shortened: **Ms. Katz, our director of sales, replied, "To increase our share of the home-appliance market, we must . . . make our products more competitive . . . ."**

As you see, in the shortened quotation two ellipses are used to show that words have been omitted from the original version. The first ellipsis has the usual three periods; the second has four periods (ellipsis + period to end sentence).

Checkup 8. Rewrite the following sentences, using ellipses to omit the words in *italics*.

1. My manager said, "Our objective is *to do everything possible* to sell, sell, sell."

   ____

2. The report said, "All of us must *be sure to take every step needed to* conserve energy." ______________________________

   ____

3. Miss Ritter promptly replied, "If we are to lower our manufacturing costs, *as has been suggested, we may find that* the quality of our products may be lessened and our sales may suffer." ______________________________

   ____

4. Mr. Flanagan said, "This new computer equipment can save time and money *for all of us in the Accounting Department and the Finance Department* if we take the time to learn to use it effectively. ______________________________

   ____

QUESTION MARKS AND EXCLAMATION POINTS

As you already know, a question mark generally ends a question, and an exclamation point ends a strong statement. In the following examples, note how question marks and exclamation points are used together with quotation marks:

"It was amazing!" Mr. Gilbert quickly yelled.
I can't believe that he said this book is "dull"!

"Where is the original copy?"
Did he say this book is "dull"?

A question mark or exclamation point goes *inside* the second quotation mark if all the words quoted make up the question or the exclamation. If the entire sentence, not just the words quoted, make up the question or exclamation, then the question mark or exclamation point goes *outside* the second quotation. (Note that periods and commas always go *inside* the second quotation.)

A question mark may be used in parentheses to show doubt. An exclamation point may be used in parentheses to show emphasis.

Brett joined our staff in 1972 (?) and was promoted shortly thereafter.
Mrs. Primm was almost 75 years old (!) when she began her cosmetic business.

Checkup 9. Add question marks or exclamation points where needed.

1. Be careful
2. We were charged $96 for cab fare to the airport
3. At age 13 she wrote her first book
4. Isn't Mr. Avery in the office today
5. Will she be able to attend a 2 o'clock meeting

REVIEW QUIZ

Add punctuation where needed.

1. Send the inquiries to Mr Swenson and Mrs Jordan.
2. The meeting with Lance Parker, Jr, was profitable.
3. Cynthia was promoted to regional manager therefore, she will be moving to Chicago.
4. We diluted the chemical with water in a 5 1 solution.
5. Note Refer to your dictionary.
6. They made an offer we accepted their bid.
7. The doctor recommended the following rest, heat, aspirin.
8. She replied this way "We explored all the alternatives. Unfortunately however we found no satisfactory solution."
9. Warning Low bridge.

10. Because these columns are narrow, type the abbreviations *ft, in, lb* and *oz,* instead of the longer words.

11. John was at his desk at 6 a.m. ( ) and left the office at the usual time.

12. In this column, type the state designations *CA, NJ, WI, MN* etc

13. He said, "I don't remember Mr. Abrams. Did I meet him at our Houston convention.

14. We received orders from Danielson's, Kenosha, Wisconsin, Rayburn's, Lexington, Kentucky, and Seely's, Clearwater, Illinois.

15. Miss Pendergast said "Do we all agree to these suggestions"

SECTION 6 WRAP-UP: Internal Punctuation Marks

The next few pages will wrap up the rules for commas, semicolons, colons, question marks, and exclamation points. Read through the reminders and review the section material briefly before doing the Spelling Exercise. The sentences you write with the spelling words will show how well you can use what you've learned in the section.

PUNCTUATION REMINDERS

The following examples are reminders of common, irritating mistakes found in everyday business correspondence. Do your best to avoid them!

Error: **A list of projects, sponsors, benefits and etc. was suggested.**

Etc. means "and so forth"; thus you should not write "*and* etc." Also, *etc.* at the end of a series should be set off by commas.

Correction: **A list of projects, sponsors, benefits, etc., was suggested.**

Error: **Jacoby, Oregon was my home.**

A state name following a city name should be set off by commas.

Correction: **Jacoby, Oregon, was my home.**

Error: **She opened her store on July 4, 1976 and has been successful ever since.**

A year number in a month/day/year date should be set off by commas.

Correction: **She opened her store on July 4, 1976, and has been successful ever since.**

Error: **It seems as if, Randy rather than his brother, has the car.**

Opposing or contrasting statements *do* need to be set off by commas—but *only* the contrasting statement, not the words that belong to the main clause.

Correction: **It seems as if Randy, rather than his brother, has the car.** The main clause is "It seems as if Randy . . . has the car.

Error: **As soon as we get the June report sales goals for the year can be revised.**

Dependent clauses that come *before* the main clause must be set off by a comma.

Correction: **As soon as we get the June report, sales goals for the year can be revised.**

SPELLING EXERCISE

Correct any misspellings in the following list of 15 words. Write your correction below each word; if a word is correctly spelled, write *C* below the word. Then for each word write a sentence as described by the instructions. Follow the example.

	WORD	SAMPLE SENTENCE
0.	bargin	(Sentence with comma) For our June sale, we are
	bargain	offering customers a special bargain.
1.	believe	(Sentence with comma) ____________
	____________	____________
2.	cemetary	(Sentence with series) ____________
	____________	____________
3.	religous	(Sentence with adjectives) ____________
	____________	____________
4.	adviseable	(Sentence with introductory phrase) ____________
	____________	____________

5. practise — (Sentence with city/state) ____________

____________ ________________________

6. similiar — (Sentence with month/day/year) ____________

____________ ________________________

7. stopt — (Sentence with direct quotation) ____________

____________ ________________________

8. absence — (Sentence with semicolon) ____________

____________ ________________________

9. excelent — (Sentence with an ellipsis) ____________

____________ ________________________

10. fourty — (Simple sentence) ____________

____________ ________________________

11. perrform — (Compound sentence) ____________

____________ ________________________

12. sevral — (Complex sentence) ____________

____________ ________________________

13. axident — (Compound-complex sentence) ____________

____________ ________________________

14. peice — (Sentence with "equal" adverb) ____________

____________ ________________________

15. facter — (Dependent clause) ____________

____________ ________________________

Special Punctuation Marks

YOUR GOALS

After finishing this section, you will be able to:

1. Use apostrophes correctly in possessives and contractions.
2. Identify titles and statements that require italics (underscoring in typing).
3. Use dashes to set off a restatement, an interrupting element, or an emphatic comment.
4. Use parentheses to set off nonessential material, and use correct punctuation marks with parentheses.
5. Correctly use quotation marks and related punctuation.
6. Use hyphens correctly in compound nouns, compound verbs, and compound adjectives.
7. Use hyphens correctly to divide words at the end of a typed line.
8. Correctly spell 15 commonly misspelled words and use 6 of them in sentences with specialized punctuation marks.

LESSON 24 Special Punctuation Marks

Special punctuation marks include apostrophes, italics, dashes, parentheses, quotation marks, and hyphens. By correctly using these special little dots and jots, you can get your message across exactly as you want to, with the same emphasis you'd use if you were talking to your reader face-to-face. Special punctuation can show a shortcut or a break in your thinking. It can help call attention to important statements. Or it can tie together words you want read as one unit. These marks are more than monotony breakers; they are power packs!

APOSTROPHES

Apostrophes are used to form the possessives of nouns. (Review Section 2 if you have questions about using an apostrophe plus *s*.)

Sue's report **Sam's appointment** **the manager's reactions**

Apostrophes also can show that letters have been left out when two words are combined into a contraction.

you're (you are)	**it's** (it is)	**don't** (do not)
they're (they are)	**we're** (we are)	**isn't** (is not)
didn't (did not)	**wouldn't** (would not)	**wasn't** (was not)

Checkup 1. Add apostrophes where needed.

1. Although I searched carefully, I couldnt find Lauras paper anywhere.
2. I couldnt go to the convention, and she wouldnt go without me.
3. Its too bad they dont import ladies clothing, not only mens clothing.

ITALICS

Italics in Titles. You've seen *italic* type throughout this book: *This is italic type*. It is used to set off titles of publications such as books, newspapers, and magazines. Italics also are used for the titles of long poems, plays, and movies.

I always read *Business Week*. **My favorite play is *The King and I*.**

Since few typewriters have italics, you usually underscore typed words that would be printed in italics.

We ran the ad in Saturday's <u>St. Paul Dispatch</u>.

Capitalization of Titles. All words in an italicized title are capitalized *except* articles, prepositions, and conjunctions that are shorter than four letters. In addition, the first and last words in the title always are capitalized, regardless of length or kind of word.

Will He Ever Give Up? ***For You and the Red Baron***

Checkup 2. Add underscores and capitals where needed. (***Reminder:*** To capitalize a lowercase letter, underscore the letter three times.)

1. We bought tickets to see the play Grease.
2. His last book, how to live successfully, was reviewed in the magazine Comments Unlimited.
3. They gave her a subscription to the toronto herald.

Italics for Emphasis. Italics or underscoring also may be used for emphasis.

She does *not* agree. **We expect that you *will* be there.**
There is *no* money left.

Caution: Keep underscoring to a minimum in business correspondence! Too much underlining will divide your reader's attention.

DASHES

Dashes work much like commas—they set apart words from the rest of the sentence. Dashes, however, show a stronger break in the flow of a sentence than commas provide. They may be used to set off restatements, interrupting elements, or emphatic comments.

Dashes With Restatements. You will remember that a restatement repeats something you've already said, only in different words. Normally you use commas to set off a restatement. Dashes make the restatement more emphatic.

If Chad—*our last hope*—does not respond, we will have no one.

↑ RESTATES CHAD

Dashes With Interrupting Elements. Dashes may be used to set off nonessential statements from the rest of the sentence. Do you see how the "side comment" interrupts the flow of this sentence and why it needs to be set apart?

If we succeed—*and why shouldn't we?*—we will be famous.

↑ INTERRUPTS SENTENCE

Dashes for Emphasis. Since dashes call attention to the material they set off, dashes provide emphasis.

Call us—today—to take advantage of this offer.

Checkup 3. Add dashes where needed.

1. We all of us need your help.
2. You're due overdue for a big raise.
3. I have that book an original first edition and I'll be glad to lend it to you.

Punctuation With Dashes. No punctuation comes *after* a dash. When words are set off by two dashes, a question mark or exclamation point may precede the second dash.

She is taking a trip around the world—did you know that?—and will not return until September.

The question mark obviously belongs to the material within the dashes, so it is placed before the second dash.

She is taking a trip around the world—imagine that!—and will not return until September.

Again, the exclamation point belongs to the words within the dashes; therefore, it goes before the second dash. Note that no punctuation goes before or after the *first* dash.

When the words set off by dashes end the sentence, drop the second dash and substitute the appropriate punctuation mark to end that sentence.

To take advantage of this offer, call us today—why not do it now?

No need for the second dash; the sentence is over. The question mark ends the sentence. Also, as you've seen, no special capitalization is needed for the words within dashes.

Checkup 4. Add dashes and other punctuation where needed.

1. They had car trouble we knew that they would and they were two hours late for the meeting.
2. I finally moved surprised? and I will start a new job next week.
3. You're to call Harris he's still in Washington as soon as you can do so.

To make a dash on the typewriter, use two hyphens, with no space before or after the dash. (Don't confuse a hyphen with a dash—it takes *two* hyphens to make one dash.)

Dashes, like exclamation points and underscoring, also should be used sparingly. If overused, these boosters become weaklings!

PARENTHESES

Parentheses are used (always in pairs) to set off nonessential material from the rest of the sentence. Whereas dashes give emphasis to set off material, parentheses de-emphasize the enclosed (parenthetical) information.

We found the data in last year's report (*page 8*).

EXTRA INFORMATION

Sally is usually (*but not always*) on time.

ADDITIONAL (NONESSENTIAL) INFORMATION

Checkup 5. Add parentheses where needed.

1. We have set aside one day Tuesday to work on our presentations.
2. A large crowd 42 persons attended the workshop.
3. My former manager she's from Alaska enjoys the climate here.

Punctuation With Parentheses. Parentheses may be used in the middle of a sentence or at the end of a sentence, or they may be used to enclose one complete, independent sentence.

In the Middle of a Sentence. Let's use a pattern to see how parentheses may be used in the *middle* of a sentence:

NEVER! SOMETIMES

Xyz xyz xyz xyz (xyz xyz xyz xyz xyz) yxz xyz xyz.

OFTEN

Never is punctuation used before or after the first parenthesis, but *sometimes* punctuation may be needed before the second parenthesis.

She is taking a trip around the world (imagine that!) and will be back in September.

She is taking a trip around the world (did you know that?) and will be back in September.

We worked long hours (from 7 a.m. to 8 p.m.) to complete the project on schedule.

As you see, an exclamation point is needed for *imagine that!* and a question mark is needed for *did you know that?* Also, periods are needed for the abbreviations *a.m.* and *p.m.*, of course. Except for such special cases, however, no punctuation is used before the second parenthesis.

Ask Mr. Jarvis (he's the head of the accounting department) to approve this payment.

Even though the parentheses enclose a complete sentence, no period is included before the second parenthesis because the sentence is part of *Ask Mr. Jarvis to approve this payment.*

Often, punctuation is needed *after* the second parenthesis. To find out, separate the parenthetical words from the rest of the sentence.

(he's on vacation)
When Mr. Jarvis returns , ask him to approve this payment.

Would you use a comma after *When Mr. Jarvis returns*? Yes. So place the comma after the second parenthesis. In other cases, you may use a semicolon or a colon or a dash—it depends on the sentence.

(about 3 or 4 percent)
Sales for June are up slightly ; however, July sales are expected to be down.

At the End of a Sentence. Here's the pattern for parenthetical copy at the end of a sentence:

Xyz xyz xyz xyz xyz (yxz yxz yxz).

As before, simply separate the parenthetical copy from the rest of the sentence:

(3 percent)
June sales are up slightly .

(3 percent)
Did you know that June sales are up slightly ?

The punctuation used depends on the sentence, not on the parentheses. Only a period, a question mark, or an exclamation point can be used, of course.

For Independent Sentences. Independent sentences—sentences that aren't attached to others—get special treatment.

(Xyz xyz xyz xyz xyz.)

Notice the capital letter that begins the independent sentence. Also, as an independent sentence, it gets its own end punctuation—a period, a question mark, or an exclamation point.

I found only one mistake. (Please see page 109.)
Unfortunately, we cannot find the original sample. (Do you have it?)
We accepted Mr. Topper's bid for the job. (It was almost *half* what we expected to pay!)

Checkup 6. Add punctuation where needed.

1. Nels was late (as usual) nevertheless, he was very helpful.
2. If you'll refer to the text (page 32) you'll find the answer.
3. I reordered these things (for the third time) envelopes, pens, and tape.
4. The first chapter in our book dealt with history. (You may want to review that material before going on) The next few chapters will discuss economics.

Caution: Don't double up on question marks or exclamation points. Rewrite the sentence, if necessary.

Okay: **The plane was late (six hours)!**
Okay: **The plane was late (six hours!).**
Wrong: **The plane was late (six hours!)!**

Checkup 7. Correct punctuation errors.

1. They reported an extremely large profit (88 percent!)!
2. For the definition of *amortize*, check your glossary (page 632.)
3. Our agency placed 62 students this year. (Our previous record was 54). We hope to increase this number next year.

QUOTATION MARKS

Quotation marks are used to show that someone's exact words are being repeated. Quotes also are used to call attention to special words, phrases, or titles.

Direct Quotation. First, be sure you understand the difference between these terms: A *direct* quotation repeats *exact* words. An *indirect* quotation does not.

Direct Quotation: **She said, "I plan to leave Thursday."**
Indirect Quotation: **She said that she planned to leave Thursday.**

Checkup 8. Write *D* after a direct quotation and *I* after an indirect quotation.

1. Milo inquired, "When shall I be there?"
2. Frances asked when she should send the letter.
3. Toni said, "I'd like an extra copy."
4. Later, another woman asked for an extra copy.

Punctuating Quotations at the End of a Sentence. As you've already noted, a comma separates a direct quotation from the rest of the sentence, and the quotation begins with a capital letter. Quotations that end a sentence do not get double punctuation.

Did she say, "Can you fix this?" Only one question mark, *inside* the second quotation.

He shouted, "Mark it 'Fragile'!" Only one exclamation point, immediately inside the second quotation. (Note the use of single quotations around *Fragile*.)

Checkup 9. Add punctuation where needed.

1. The administrator said The report has already been submitted
2. Henry exclaimed Here they come
3. Did she say May I have a duplicate

Punctuating Quotations at the Beginning of a Sentence. A quotation at the beginning of a sentence starts with a capital, of course. Usually, a comma separates it from the rest of the sentence.

"We know she'll finish the project on time," Martha said.

But a question mark replaces the comma if the quotation is a question. An exclamation point replaces the comma if the quotation is an exclamation. Either one will be placed *inside* the second quotation.

"She'll finish it on time!" Martha exclaimed.
"Will she finish it on time?" Martha asked.

Checkup 10. Add punctuation where needed.

1. Who is the treasurer Patricia asked
2. Nobody seems to know Barry replied
3. I insist that you follow directions Mike ordered

Punctuating Split Quotations. When you split a quotation into two parts, do not begin the second part with a capital letter.

"You need to remember," she continued, "that we are in agreement."

NO CAPITAL

Of course, this does not apply when two independent sentences are quoted and split. In this case, the two statements would be separated by a period, and the second sentence would begin with a capital letter.

"We want you to head this department. Do you want to work with us?"

PERIOD SEPARATES TWO STATEMENTS CAPITAL

CAPITAL

"My answer is right," she insisted. "Yours is wrong."

PERIOD SEPARATES TWO STATEMENTS

Checkup 11. Add punctuation and capitals where needed.

1. If you can't tell me now she said please call me later today.
2. The store is now closed he said it will be open tomorrow at 8 a.m.
3. Have you called the supplier she asked our order should be ready by now

4. As Ms. Kirschner said we must have all the costs no later than Monday

5. If you are not sure of the list price ask Mr. Hobson Elaine suggested

Punctuating Longer Quotations. When several sentences are quoted, place quotation marks only at the beginning and end of the entire quotation, not around each sentence. ***Reminder:*** Sometimes long, formal quotations may be introduced by a colon, rather than by a comma.

INTRODUCTORY COLON

The committee report read as follows: "We recommend a provisional license for two years. Renewal will depend upon satisfactory performance during that time."

When quoting more than one paragraph, place quotation marks at the beginning of *each* paragraph *but only at the end of the final paragraph*, not at the end of each paragraph.

The chairperson responded this way: "The matter was thoroughly discussed. Since all the Task Force members were in attendance, we were able to agree on definite recommendations.

"First, we suggest more frequent meetings. The frequency of meetings appears to be of prime importance to most participants.

"Next, we recommend a formal survey of our customers. This survey . . . would yield some valuable marketing information."

Notice the quotation marks at the beginning of each paragraph and at the end of only the final paragraph. Notice also the ellipsis marks in the last sentence. It tells you that some words are omitted from the original statement.

Checkup 12. Add punctuation where needed.

The president of the company made this announcement:

I am delighted to inform you that we are expanding employees' benefits effective January 1.

First of all, medical coverage is now paid entirely by the company. This applies to each employee and his or her dependents.

Second, a dental plan is now available for employees and their dependents at a very low cost. The details of this plan will be announced within the next two weeks.

Third, the employees' retirement plan has been revised to give you greater coverage at a lower monthly cost.

Complete details will be given in a special bulletin that we will distribute early next week.

As an alternative to using quotation marks, long quotations (three or more typed lines) may be indented and single-spaced, with the quotation marks omitted completely.

The brochure gives this useful information on attendance:

> **Tuition is free, and living is inexpensive. Student loans and grants for supplies and subsistence, both federal and state, are readily available to eligible students. In addition, assistance in obtaining housing is provided through the student personnel office.**

Quoted Words and Phrases. In addition to indicating a direct quotation, quotation marks may be used for special terms such as "Confidential," "Registered," and "Rush," and for slang terms or for words used ironically.

Slang Term: **She thinks he's "cool."**
Irony: **His so-called "assistant" left early today.**

Quoted Titles Within a Publication. We said earlier that titles of books, magazines, newspapers, and other separate publications are printed in *italics* (underscored in typing). But for titles of chapters, articles, and stories *within* a book or periodical, use quotation marks.

Story Within a Book: **We read Poe's "The Cask of Amontillado" in *American Short Stories.***

Article Within a Magazine: **The article "How to Build a Solar Unit" appeared in a recent issue of *Mechanics Illustrated.***

Checkup 13. Add punctuation where needed.

1. Please mark the packages Fragile.
2. I write the column Daily Trends in the Crayville News.
3. Their supposedly fresh salads were sadly wilted.

Commas and Periods With Quotations. Commas or periods following quotations always, *always,* fall *inside* the quotation marks.

INSIDE
↓
"Please tell me," she pleaded.
Although the package was marked "Fragile," it was damaged.
We marked the letter "Rush."
Poisons are labeled with an "X."

Semicolons and Colons With Quotations. Semicolons and colons, on the other hand, always, *always* go *outside* the quotation marks.

OUTSIDE
↓
The brochure states, "Make an appointment"; nevertheless, they arrived unannounced.

The following literary devices are evident in Shelley's "Ode to the West Wind": personification, simile, and paradox.

Question Marks and Exclamation Points With Quotations. Question marks and exclamation points fall either inside or outside the quotes, depending on whether they relate only to the quoted material or to the entire sentence.

Inside (relates to quote only):	**He asked, "Will they be early?"**
Inside (relates to quote only):	**Her reply was, "Forget it!"**
Outside (relates to entire sentence):	**Is he really "Okay"?**
Outside (relates to entire sentence):	**You'll be amazed at my "new image"!**

Checkup 14. Add punctuation where needed.

1. I ordered these items from the newspaper's "Mailorder Section" slippers, hosiery, handkerchiefs, and perfume.
2. What does he consider "home"
3. Fred calls her "Mrs. Ames" but Janice calls her "Sharon"
4. We had to read the article "Safe Driving" furthermore, we had to define the word "safe"

That takes care of apostrophes, italics, dashes, parentheses, and quotation marks. Let's take a minute to review how they're used.

MARK	USE
Apostrophes:	**To show possession or omitted letters in contractions.**
Italics:	**To indicate titles of separate publications or special emphasis.**
Dashes:	**To set off restatements, interrupting elements, or emphatic comments.**
Parentheses:	**To set off nonessential material.**
Quotation Marks:	**To indicate direct quotations, special words or phrases, or titles within a publication.**

Can you correctly punctuate sentences using these marks? If you're not sure, read through the material once again.

REVIEW QUIZ

Add punctuation where needed in the following sentences, and circle each addition. Circle and correct any improper use of special punctuation. Write a C after any correct sentences. An example is given.

0. Kahlil Gibran said, "Your house is your larger body."
1. These are the time's that try mens souls said Thomas Paine.
2. Paine also stated What we obtain too cheap, we esteem too lightly.

3. The selection has to be made you know it and it has to be made soon.
4. Send in your order hurry before its too late.
5. Stephen Foster wrote Old Folks at Home, Anthonys favorite song.
6. I seldom read the Letters to the Editor section of The Downtown News, nevertheless, I enjoyed it in last weeks issue.
7. The following emotions were aroused by Churchills famous "Blood, Sweat, and Tears" address hope, dedication, and patriotism.
8. Snow, ice, and cold weather all of which I detest are common during Minnesotas winter season.
9. The parade started on time (for a change) but the band was late.
10. When we get together again—soon, I hope—we will discuss your offer.

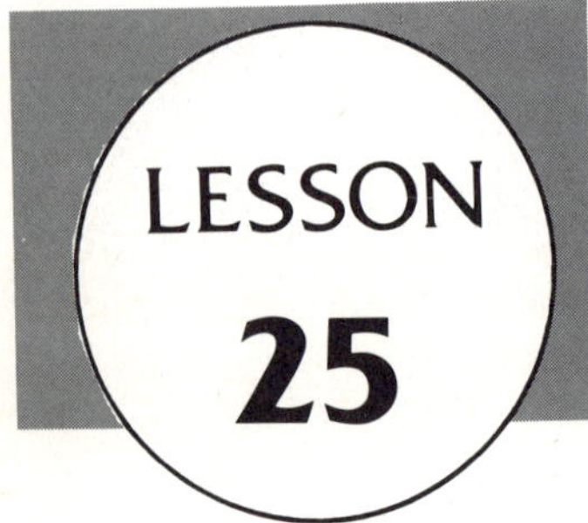

Hyphens

A hyphen (-) links individual words together into one unit, either temporarily or permanently. In addition, a hyphen at the end of a typed line shows that the last word has been split (because there wasn't room for all of it on that line) and that the word continues on the next line.

LINKING COMPOUND UNITS

Prefixes and Suffixes. Many of our common words are a combination of a basic "root" word and a prefix or suffix. A prefix comes before the root word, and a suffix comes after. Remember that *pre* means "before."

ROOT WORD ROOT WORD
↓ ↓
re/align **re/design**
↑ ↑
PREFIX MEANING "AGAIN"

ROOT WORD ROOT WORD

pink/ish **boy/ish**

SUFFIX MEANING "LIKE" OR "SOMEWHAT"

SUFFIX MEANING "WHEEL"

uni/cycle **bi/cycle** **tri/cycle**

PREFIXES MEANING "ONE," "TWO," AND "THREE"

Most prefixes and suffixes are combined with root words without a hyphen: *preempt*, *reevaluate*, *coordinate*, and *cooperate*.

However, if spelling without a hyphen makes a word likely to be mistaken for another word, you should use a hyphen. Notice the difference in meaning in the following similar words.

recover (meaning regain)
re-cover (meaning cover again)

coop (a cage)
co-op (a shortened form of *cooperative*)

One special prefix should be noted. With few exceptions (*selfish, selfless, selfhood,* and *selfsame*), the prefix *self* requires a hyphen.

self-composed **self-loading** **self-restraint** **self-defeating**

Remember: Your dictionary is your best spelling guide!

Checkup 1. Add or remove hyphens as needed.

1. Have you considered recovering your sofa and chairs?
2. We're supposed to pre-register for the conference so that they can re-evaluate attendance estimates.
3. Non-essential material is usually set off by commas.

Compound Numbers and Fractions. Spelled-out compound numbers between twenty and one hundred are hyphenated, as are written-out fractions.

twenty-six **thirty-two** **one-fifth** **three-quarters**

Checkup 2. Add hyphens where needed.

1. My twenty first birthday was last week.
2. Only three fourths of the staff arrived on time.
3. There were thirty two applicants.

Compound Nouns, Verbs, and Adjectives. Compounds may be written in three ways: with a space between the words, with no space between the words, or with a hyphen between the words. There are so many compounds, however, that not all are listed in the dictionary. Therefore, you will have to do some thinking to decide how to write certain compounds.

Compound Nouns. Compound nouns may be written with a space between the words, no space between them, or a hyphen between them.

this punch bowl **a trademark** **a pick-me-up**

Use your dictionary to make sure your choice is correct. If the compound isn't listed in the dictionary, write the compound with a space between the words. Note, however, that compound nouns such as *secretary-treasurer, dinner-dance,* and *counselor-friend* are always written with hyphens.

Checkup 3. Add or remove hyphens as needed.

1. The table-cloth was old and worn.
2. The toll keeper collected my fee at the tollbridge.
3. The field was flooded with moon beams.

Compound Verbs. Most compound verbs are spelled with a hyphen or with no space between them.

to fast-freeze **to rubber-stamp** **to proofread** **to sidetrack**

However, verb and adverb combinations are written as two separate words.

to make up **to buy out** **to cash in** **to mark up**

Again, always use your dictionary to make sure you're correct.

Checkup 4. Add or remove hyphens as needed.

1. They can quick freeze almost anything you bring-in.
2. Don't let them back-slide into old-fashioned methods.
3. Shall we blind-fold the contestants before we begin?

Compound Adjectives. Here's where thinking is a must—with compound adjectives. A compound adjective is a two-word (or a three-word) unit that modifies a noun. Follow your dictionary to see whether a space, no space, or a hyphen is needed between the words.

***real estate* tax** ***farsighted* advice** ***quick-tempered* disposition**

Your dictionary does not list all the possible compound adjectives, however. In addition, some of the compound adjectives are hyphenated only when they come before the noun modified; after the noun, they may not need hyphens.

BEFORE THE NOUN	AFTER THE NOUN
a *4-gallon* drum	**a drum that holds *4 gallons***
a *well-written* story	**a story that is *well written***
a *low-tension* cable	**a cable that has *low tension***
a *two-year* lease	**a lease that lasts *two years***

After the noun, there is no need to hold these words together with a hyphen because the words are in normal order. That's the reason for the hyphen before the noun: to hold together words that are *not* in normal order.

There are compound adjectives that are hyphenated both before the noun and after the noun:

BEFORE THE NOUN	AFTER THE NOUN
an *old-fashioned* scene	**a scene that is *old-fashioned***
a *time-consuming* project	**a project that is *time-consuming***
a *right-handed* player	**a player who is *right-handed***

The compounds *old-fashioned, time-consuming,* and *right-handed* are not in normal order; they need hyphens to hold them together.

As you see, then, your dictionary usually will list compound adjectives that are spelled with no space or with a space, but you must do some thinking for the hyphenated compounds.

Troublesome Compounds. You already saw that *real estate* was not hyphenated. Let's look at some other compounds that are not hyphenated:

a *high school* play
your *life insurance* premiums
a *9 percent* increase
a *Los Angeles* firm
the *Supreme Court* ruling
her *social security* payment

There is no possibility of confusing these compounds. Therefore, no hyphen is needed. Other compounds that need no hyphens are those which have *ly* adverbs modifying an adjective.

a *highly respected* attorney
a *completely new* agenda
a *thoroughly checked* engine
a *modestly successful* business

Here, the *ly* adverbs *highly, completely, thoroughly,* and *modestly* can modify only the adjectives that follow: *respected, new, checked,* and *successful.* No hyphen is needed because there is no possibility of confusion. Do not use a hyphen to join an *ly* adverb to an adjective.

Of course, beware of two equal adjectives that modify a noun. When two adjectives both modify the same noun, they should not be hyphenated; they generally are separated by a comma.

a *bright, cheerful* room **his *dirty, cluttered* desk** **the *long, slow* drive**

"Hanging" Hyphens. In a series of hyphenated terms, repetition can be avoided by using the hyphen as follows:

We need *6-, 10-,* and *15-quart* drums.
She has *12-, 18-,* and *36-inch* rulers.

The word *quart* is understood after *6-* and *10-*, and the word *inch* is understood after *12-* and *18-*. Note how the commas are used.

Checkup 5. Add or remove hyphens as needed.

1. The soft spoken teen-ager taperecorded the entire work-shop.
2. We bought a sturdy-comfortable-rocking-chair.
3. The bid came from a highly-recommended contractor.

Age and Numbers. Compound adjectives expressing age require hyphens, as do other combinations involving numbers.

sixty-year-old man **a $23-a-night room**

Remember: Only the compound adjective is hyphened, not the noun it modifies.

Percent and Money. No hyphens are used in expressions such as these:

a 15 percent raise *(**not:** a 15-percent)*
a $6 billion debt *(**not:** a $6-billion)*

Checkup 6. Add or remove hyphens as needed.

1. The author was a sixteen year-old-girl.
2. We had a 16-percent reduction in absenteeism last year.
3. Please buy 13, 15, and 20 cent stamps.
4. Mrs. Angus has a reputation for being a cost conscious manager.

END-OF-LINE HYPHENS

When you're typing and you must break a word at the end of a line, precisely where do you divide that word? There are rules governing word division, and you must know them. The following summary will be helpful, but for a complete discussion on word division, refer to the front of your dictionary or to a reference manual.

Natural Breaks. Whenever possible, of course, break a compound between the two words. Separate prefixes and suffixes, and divide between double consonants.

home- owner	**sales- clerk**	**goal- keeper**	**bank- book**
pre- clude	**multi- media**	**semi- annual**	**sub- division**
nation- wide	**process- ing**	**entertain- ment**	**peace- ful**
suc- cess	**occur- rence**	**col- lection**	**recom- mendation**

However, do not break double consonants that signal the end of complete words—for example, *roll-ing* (not *rol-ling*), *pull-over* (not *pul-lover*), and so on.

Of course, between-syllable breaks are natural breaks:

gradu- ate	**citi- zen**	**cus- tody**

In the above examples, note that it is better to break *graduate* between the consecutive vowels because each vowel is sounded. Note, too, that it is better to break *citizen* after the vowel (*citi-zen*), rather than before (*cit-izen*).

Checkup 7. Rewrite each word, using a hyphen to show the end-of-line break.

1. criticism ____________ 4. personnel ____________
2. sanitation ____________ 5. convenience ____________
3. settlement ____________ 6. bookkeeping ____________

Unnatural Breaks. There are some don'ts to remember when dividing words at the end of a line.

DON'T . . .	FOR EXAMPLE . . .
1. Break one-syllable words.	**quite, there, rushed**
2. Divide contractions.	**won't, isn't, hasn't**
3. Divide abbreviations.	**UNICEF, NBC, USMC**
4. Break words shorter than five letters.	**redo, atom, upon, item**
5. Leave one letter (plus the hyphen) at the end of a line.	**i- dealism** **e- lude**
6. Carry over only one or two letters to the next line (with or without punctuation).	**embas- sy** **cred- it**

Also, if possible, avoid breaking names and numbers. However, if you must break names and numbers, divide them as follows:

$632,- 000	**1,876,- 050**	**Jeremy S. Snyder, Ph.D.**	**Dr. K. L. Rosen**

Checkup 8. The following words and numbers must be divided. Use a hyphen to show the breaks for each in the space provided.

1. statement ____________
2. industry ____________
3. complete ____________
4. specifications ____________
5. material ____________
6. corporation ____________
7. 9,300,424 ____________
8. recognize ____________
9. distribution ____________
10. Lane P. Ryan, R.N. ____________
11. original ____________
12. electronic ____________

Review the rules for end-of-line hyphenation. Be sure you know the "don'ts"!

REVIEW QUIZ

Part 1. Correct the following sentences by adding or deleting hyphens. Circle each error. Write a C after each correct sentence. Follow the example.

0. A successful sales representative must be (self-disciplined) and (co-operative.)
1. Students may buy supplies from the local coop book-store.
2. A re-imbursement form must be pre-pared in duplicate.
3. The twenty second amendment was read by the secretary treasurer.
4. I hope that you have a pleasant-safe flight to Florida.
5. Bernard had an extremely-bad head cold, and he suffered a gr-
   eat deal from stuffed-up sinuses.
6. I collect 5, 10, and 25 cent coins.
7. My 88 year old grandfather is still active and alert.
8. We reserved two $35-a-night rooms.
9. Over one half of our members are non-licensed.
10. Some areas of the room must be re-cleaned and repainted.

Part 2. Fill in the blanks in the following sentences.

1. A hyphened word at the end of a line must have at least ____________ letters.
2. On the next line, at least ____________ letters must be carried over.

3. When dividing words at the end of the line, *don't*:

a. ______________________________

b. ______________________________

c. ______________________________

d. ______________________________

e. ______________________________

f. ______________________________

SECTION 7 WRAP-UP: Special Punctuation Marks

We have now covered the various punctuation marks. To help tie it all together, review the rules and exercises. You'll have to be able to spot incorrect usage, as well as use different kinds of punctuation when you complete the Spelling Exercise. Let's see how well you can do.

PUNCTUATION REMINDERS

Notice the following common, irritating mistakes. Do your best to avoid them.

Error: **I have a copy of "The Complete Works Of Shakespeare."**

Books and other separate publications are printed in *italics* (underscored in typing), while articles, chapters, and parts of a publication are enclosed in quotation marks. Also, articles, conjunctions, and prepositions under four letters are not capitalized, except for the first or last word of the title.

Correction: **I have a copy of *The Complete Works of Shakespeare.***

Error: **I knew the auditor was coming, (didn't you) so I prepared carefully.**

With parentheses, the normal punctuation is "postponed" so that it follows the second parenthesis. Also, a question within parentheses must have its own question mark.

Correction: **I knew the auditor was coming (didn't you?), so I prepared carefully.**

Error: **The sign read "Beware of the Dog".**

Periods and commas *always* fall inside the second quotation mark; colons and semicolons *always* fall outside the second quotation mark. Question marks and exclamation points can fall either inside or outside, depending on whether they belong to the quoted material only or to the whole sentence.

Correction: **The sign read "Beware of the Dog."**

Error: **The applicant will receive a two year license.**

Most compound adjectives are joined with a hyphen.

Correction: **The applicant will receive a two-year license.**

Error: **Our New-York office reported an 18-percent increase in sales.**

Among the compound adjectives that do not require hyphens are proper adjectives (such as *New York*) and very commonly used compounds (such as *18 percent, real estate,* and *high school*).

Correction: **Our New York office reported an 18 percent increase in sales.**

SPELLING EXERCISE

Correct each misspelled word in the following list by writing your correction in the space below each word. If a word is correctly spelled, write *C* below the word. Then, using each word, write a sample sentence as instructed. Follow the example.

	WORD	SAMPLE SENTENCE
0.	discused discussed	(Sentence with apostrophe) At yesterday's meeting, we discussed our strategies.
1.	industrie ________	(Sentence with quotations) ________
2.	perminent ________	(Sentence with dashes) ________
3.	accomodation ________	(Sentence with parentheses) ________
4.	apolagy ________	(Sentence with hyphen) ________

5. belligernse ____________ (Sentence with question mark) ____________

6. sucess ____________ (Sentence with semicolon) ____________

7. rehearsal ____________ (Sentence with colon) ____________

8. interuption ____________ (Sentence with apostrophe) ____________

9. expence ____________ (Sentence with quotations) ____________

10. fasination ____________ (Sentence with two commas) ____________

11. sissors ____________ (Sentence with dashes) ____________

12. compitition ____________ (Sentence with exclamation mark) ____________

13. necesity ____________ (Sentence with hyphen) ____________

14. sophomore ____________ (Sentence with two commas) ____________

15. temprament ____________ (Sentence with parentheses) ____________

Agreement, Parallelism, and Numbers

YOUR GOALS

After studying this section, you will be able to:

1. Recognize and correct errors in agreement.
2. Recognize and correct errors in parallelism.
3. Correctly express numbers in business correspondence.
4. Correctly spell 15 commonly misspelled words, using them in sentences that show agreement of sentence parts, parallelism, and correct number usage.

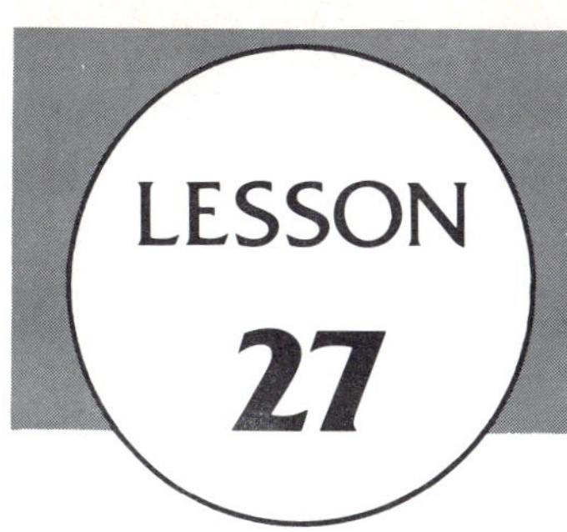

LESSON 27 Agreement

Congratulations! You've now studied all the main patterns you'll need to shape your messages. You've identified and used different kinds of words, phrases, clauses, and sentences. You've seen how punctuation marks serve as road signs for your readers. And you've seen the importance of having all sentence parts "agree," so that your messages will be clear and effective. That's what this lesson is all about—agreement.

Since we've already mentioned agreement of sentence parts in a number of lessons, some of these examples will be just review.

PRONOUN AGREEMENT

Personal Pronouns. A personal pronoun must agree with its referent in both number and sex. It also must agree with the verb. You will remember that a referent is the noun that the pronoun refers to and replaces.

> ***Gertrude* says that *she* has *her* speech prepared for the meeting that will be held in the conference room next Wednesday.**

Do you see that *she* and *her* are pronouns? They refer to the noun *Gertrude* (the referent). Because the noun *Gertrude* is singular and female, the pronouns that refer to it also must be singular and female: *she* and *her.* In other words, they must *agree.*

The sentence also shows another kind of agreement—agreement of subjects and verbs. In *Gertrude says,* the verb *says* is third-person singular, to agree with *Gertrude.* In *she has,* the verb *has* is third-person singular, to agree with *she.*

Now let's look at a similar sentence with a plural referent, plural pronouns, and plural verbs:

***Matt and Tim* say that *they* have *their* speeches prepared for the meeting.**

Here, the plural pronouns *they* and *their* refer to the plural (compound) subject *Matt and Tim.* The pronouns and their referent *agree.*

Note, too, the plural verbs *say* and *have.* These verbs agree with their subjects.

Checkup 1. Fill in the blanks with the appropriate personal pronouns, and underline the correct verbs in parentheses. (Make sure that your pronouns *agree* with their referents and your verbs *agree* with their subjects.)

1. Mick and Harriet (has, have) moved into __________ new house, and __________ (am, is, are) busy decorating.
2. Ms. VanGilder (is, are) treasurer of the corporation, which __________ joined in 1976.
3. Both Mrs. Stein and __________ husband (was, were) at the press conference to announce __________ daughter's candidacy.

Who. The pronoun *who* can be used to refer to various singular or plural nouns and pronouns. Therefore, the verb used to agree with *who* depends on the *referent:*

It is Mary who *is* always on schedule. Because *who* refers to *Mary,* the verb *is* agrees with *who* (*Mary . . . is, who is*).

It is the supervisors who *are* complaining about this. Here, *who* refers to the plural *supervisors,* so the plural *are* is correct (*supervisors . . . are, who are*).

It is I who *am* responsible for this error. Here, *who* refers to *I,* so *am* is the correct verb.

Don't be fooled by interrupters! Always find the referent for *who* and you'll be sure to choose a verb that agrees.

It is Jeff, not the supervisors, who *is* asking for a budget change. *Who* refers to *Jeff,* not to *supervisors,* thus *is* is correct (*Jeff . . . is, who is*).

Annette now works for Mrs. Browley, one of the new managers, who *is* the head of our Dallas office. *Who* refers to *Mrs. Browley,* not to *managers,* so *is* is the correct verb (*Mrs. Browley . . . is, who is*).

In matching *who* with a pronoun and a verb, be sure that you have picked out the right subject. Remember that interrupters do not contain the subject.

Checkup 2. Underline the correct pronouns and verbs.

1. Ed and Kay (claim, claims) that (he, she, they), not Francis, (am, is, are) the winners.
2. I think that she, rather than you, (have been, has been) chosen as the chairperson.

A Special Problem. Notice the difference in the following sentences:

Vanda is one of the accountants who *have* invested *their* money in company stock.

Vanda is the only one of the accountants who *has* invested *her* money in company stock.

Why does the first sentence use *have* and *their* to agree with *accountants*, and why does the second sentence use *has* and *her* to agree with *the only one*? Simple: In the first sentence, Vanda is "one of *several people* who . . . ." *Who* refers to *people* or *accountants* or whatever *plural* word precedes it. But in the second sentence, Vanda is clearly "the *only one* of several people who . . . ." The meaning of "the *only one*" is clearly singular.

When you see "*one of* . . . who," you'll know that *who* is plural. When you see "the *only one* . . . who," you'll know that *who* is singular.

Checkup 3. Underline the correct verbs.

1. Colleen is one of our employees who (is, are) always prompt.
2. John is the only one of our sales representatives who (work, works) in the Wyoming area.

VERB AGREEMENT

With Subjects Joined by *Or, Either . . . Or, Neither . . . Nor.* When two subjects are joined by *or, either . . . or, neither . . . nor,* or *not only . . . but also,* the verb agrees with the second subject:

Either Pat or her *partners are* in the store. *Are* agrees with the second subject, *partners.*

Either her partners or *Pat is* in the store. *Is* agrees with the second subject, *Pat.*

Neither the employees nor the *employers were* satisfied with the contract. *Were* agrees with the second subject, *employers.*

Not only Judd but also *Caryl is* a government auditor. *Is* agrees with *Caryl.*

Mr. Turin or *Ms. Rome was* scheduled to speak. *Was* agrees with *Ms. Rome.*

Dr. Fierst or *I am* to speak first. *Am* agrees with *I.*

Checkup 4. Underline the correct verbs.

1. Not only the secretaries but also Greg (need, needs) help.
2. Neither those houses nor this one (is, are) for sale.
3. Either our boss or our supervisors (have, has) the final agenda.

With Collective Nouns. A collective noun stands for a group of people or a collection of things. If the collective noun is spoken about as one unit acting together, it takes a singular verb. If the collective noun is spoken about as separate units acting individually, it takes a plural verb.

The grand jury *is* now facing *its* toughest case. *Is* and *its*, both singular, to show action as a group.

The grand jury *are* arguing whether *they* should hand up an indictment. *Are* and *they*, both plural, to show that the jury members are acting individually.

Checkup 5. Underline the collective nouns. Then rewrite the sentences to correct any errors in pronoun and verb usage. Write *OK* if a sentence has no errors.

1. The troupe always gives its best performance at the matinee show. ______

 ____

2. I told the team to empty its lockers and to sign out before it leaves. ______

 ____

3. Our staff is standing by its contract demands. ______________

 ____

With *A Number/The Number.* *A number* is always plural. *The number* is always singular.

Singular: ***The number* of people involved *is* small.**
Plural: ***A number* of people *are* involved.**

With Phrases and Clauses as Subjects. When a phrase or a clause is used as the subject of a sentence, it is singular and requires a singular verb.

Phrase as Subject: ***Running several miles every morning is* her main source of exercise.**

The phrase *Running several miles every morning* is a noun—a singular noun—and it requires a singular verb, *is.* What pronoun would you use as a substitute for *Running several miles every morning*? If you said *It*, you're correct!

***It is* her main source of exercise.**

***Running in the morning* and *swimming in the evening are* her favorite exercises.** *Are* is correct: *They are* her favorite exercises.

Clause as Subject: ***Whatever you do is* fine with us.** *Whatever you do* is used as a singular noun here; it is the subject of the singular verb *is.* (*It* is fine with us.)

Checkup 6. Underline the correct verbs.

1. Writing reports (cause, causes) me a problem.
2. The number of restaurants in our vicinity (is, are) low.
3. I know that a number of people (was, were) planning to come.

ed as subjects, percentages and frac-
ding on the noun to which they refer.

***was* due to theft.**

n *loss*; thus a singular verb (*was*) is
n be substituted: *Some of our loss*

stomers *are* over 65.

n *customers*, a plural verb (*are*) is

active.
(take, takes) vacation in July or

was, were) damaged.

ful not to let interrupting phrases
ubject and its verb. Look for the
. Then choose your verb.

The new *policy, with its many technicalities, is* unfair.

INTERRUPTING PHRASE

Clearly, you are saying *"The policy . . . is unfair."*

A *list of potential jobs is* enclosed for your use.

INTERRUPTING PHRASE

Obviously, *A list . . . is* is correct.

Checkup 8. Underline the correct verbs. Box the interrupting phrases.

1. A copy of the errors (was, were) sent to her.
2. The last parts of the book (is, are) unclear.
3. My day, in spite of interruptions, (has, have) been productive.

With Indefinite Pronouns. *Caution:* There's an exception to this rule about ignoring interrupting material. Do you remember the six indefinite pronouns we studied that depend on the following phrase for their number? Let's review. When using *none, any, some, more, most,* or *all* of something as the subject, you *do* need to consider the interrupting phrase; otherwise you won't know whether you need a singular or a plural verb. These words work just like the percentages and fractions we just went over. Here's a reminder:

None of the *boys are* willing.
None of the *cake is* gone.

Checkup 9. Underline the correct verbs.

1. If any of the nurses (is, are) here, please let me know.
2. Some of the assignment (is, are) already complete.
3. All of the roofs (was, were) covered with snow.

Now you should be able to use subjects, pronouns, and verbs that *agree*. Are you ready for a review quiz?

REVIEW QUIZ

Underline the correct pronouns and verbs.

1. Yes, it was Perry and Frank who (was, were) appealing (his, her, its, their) case.
2. If any of the supervisors (want, wants) help, (he, they) need only ask.
3. It's the jury members, not the judge, who (is, are) responsible.
4. He is one of the messengers who (deliver, delivers) to us regularly.
5. Most of the addresses (is, are) outdated.
6. Perhaps Mr. Frankel, not the assistants, (is, are) leaving.
7. Do you think it's he who (is, are) to blame for these errors?
8. Sam is the only one of the managers who (has, have) (his, their) sales forecast ready.
9. Either the editor in chief or you (is, are) going to the press conference.
10. Brenda is the only one of the models who (do, does) not work for an agency.
11. Exercising vigorously for several hours (is, are) the way he stays slim.
12. Two-thirds of you people (is, are) on the list.
13. Sometimes up to 79 percent of our membership (respond, responds) to these mailings.
14. Rubber strips, not plastic sheeting, (is, are) most effective.
15. Mrs. Donnelly, not one of her assistants, (has, have) the key to the conference room.
16. Neither you nor I (are, is, am) ready for retirement.
17. A number of the phrases (was, were) deleted.
18. The latest catalog of men's and women's fashions (is, are) enclosed.
19. The number of dropouts (has, have) declined.

Parallelism and Dangling Constructions

PARALLELISM

Agreement of sentence parts, which you've just studied, is important in making your messages clear and effective. A special kind of agreement to watch for is parallelism. In writing, *parallelism* means that grouped words, phrases, or clauses are similar and matched.

Items in a Series. When a series of items is listed, the items should be parallel—that is, they should be identical constructions, not a mixture of different structures. This rule applies whether you're giving a series of words, phrases, or clauses.

I like *hiking, camping,* and *swimming.*
hiking = *camping* = *swimming* (All are verbal nouns.)
I like *to hike, to camp,* and *to swim.*
to hike = *to camp* = *to swim* (All are infinitives.)
or: **I like to *hike, camp,* and *swim.***

Jim enjoys hiking, Lorraine enjoys camping, **and** *Vera enjoys swimming.* All are clauses.

Give *a copy to Mr. Taylor, one to Mrs. Smyth,* **and** *one to me.* All are parallel direct objects of the verb *Give.*

The items in each series are matched. But *don't* mix different items, as in the following sentences:

Wrong: **I like** *hiking, camping,* **and** *to swim.* Two verbal nouns plus an infinitive.

Wrong: **I like** *to hike, to camp,* **and** *swimming.* Two infinitives plus a verbal noun.

Let's look at another nonparallel example:

Wrong: **Rose is** *young, athletic,* **and** *is intelligent.*

Young and *athletic* are both adjectives, but *is intelligent* is not. It isn't parallel to the adjectives. Delete *is.*

Correct: **Rose is** *young, athletic,* **and** *intelligent.*

Now the items in the series are parallel—all are adjectives: *young, athletic, intelligent.*

Checkup 1. Rewrite the sentences to correct any errors in parallelism.

1. August was cold, windy, and was wet. ____________________

____

2. The campers looked for firewood, for kindling, and wanted a dry spot. ___

____

3. In his spare time, Kevin likes to watch TV, read a magazine, or some guitar practice. ____________________________

____

Paired Conjunctions. When using paired conjunctions (*either . . . or, neither . . . nor*), be sure you place the conjunctions so that the items joined are equal. Notice the equality in the following structures.

We will meet either *my sister* **or** *her husband.*
NOUN PHRASE NOUN PHRASE

Each conjunction is followed by a noun phrase. Therefore, the structures are parallel.

We will meet either *my sister* **or** *yours.*

Yours is a pronoun, so it is considered parallel to the noun phrase *my sister.* (Here, *yours* means "your sister.")

We will either *meet my sister* or *call her husband.*

VERB PHRASE — VERB PHRASE

In this sentence each conjunction is followed by a verb phrase. But notice what happens when you put the conjunction *either* in the wrong place.

Wrong: **We will either *meet my sister* or *her husband.***

VERB PHRASE — NOUN PHRASE

In this sentence *either* is followed by a verb phrase, but *or* is followed by a noun phrase. The parts are not parallel.

Let's take another example, using *neither . . . nor.*

The plane neither *goes to Chicago* nor *lands in Omaha.*

VERB PHRASE — VERB PHRASE

The verb phrase following the conjunctions are equal.

The plane goes to neither *Chicago* nor *Omaha.*

NOUN — NOUN

The conjunctions are followed by equal nouns. But look what happens when we put the conjunction in the wrong place.

Wrong: **The plane neither *goes to Chicago* nor *to Omaha.***

VERB PHRASE — PREPOSITIONAL PHRASE

In this sentence the phrases are not equal. We do *not* have parallelism.

Checkup 2. Rewrite the sentences to correct any errors in parallelism.

1. I will either need to join a car pool or buy a car. ____________________

____

2. They either must improve production or reduce staff. ____________________

____

3. The clerks neither want to stay late nor come early. ____________________

____

Parallel Comparisons. Items being compared must be parallel.

June's sales* were better than *July's sales.

June's sales and *July's sales* are obviously parallel. But a problem arises when we leave out one or more words in the comparison.

June's sales* were better than *July's.

The sentence is still correct. It is understood that *July's* means "July's sales." The error usually occurs when the possessive *July's* becomes *July.*

Wrong: ***June's sales* were better than *July.***

Literally, this compares *sales* with *July*—a comparison that makes no sense. *Sales* must be compared with *sales.*

Let's see another example.

Wrong: ***This week's attendance* is better than *last week.***
Right: ***This week's attendance* is better than *last week's.***

To see whether a possessive is needed, mentally supply the missing noun.

Checkup 3. Rewrite the sentences to correct any errors in parallelism.

1. The last manager's experience was more extensive than this manager. ______

______

2. My father's business is more successful than my brother. ______

______

3. Her office is more crowded than Roger. ______

______

DANGLING PHRASES AND CLAUSES

Sometimes a modifying phrase or clause is put in the wrong place, making that phrase or clause describe the wrong noun. Such a misplaced modifier is said to *dangle*, because it doesn't have an appropriate noun to hook up to. It just dangles in space by itself.

Phrase With Participle. First, let's look at a modifying phrase that's in the right place. This phrase contains a participle (an adjective derived from a verb).

***Having nothing better to do*, Curt turned on the TV.**

Here, the modifying phrase (in italics) correctly describes *Curt.* (The participle is *having.*) Now let's make the phrase dangle.

Dangling: ***Having nothing better to do*, the TV was turned on.**

Now the phrase modifies *TV*! The modifying phrase describes the wrong subject. Obviously, it wasn't the TV that had "nothing better to do." The modifying phrase should describe the subject of the sentence. Also, the modifying phrase should be as close to the subject as possible.

Dangling: ***Walking quickly toward the elevator*, the carpet tripped Ms. Dodd.**

Obviously, the carpet wasn't "walking quickly toward the elevator"!

Right: ***Walking quickly toward the elevator*, Ms. Dodd tripped on the carpet.**

The participles you've seen (*having* and *walking*) are present participles; they always end in *ing*. Past participles, too, are used as adjectives and therefore can dangle.

Dangling: ***Retyped and printed in color*, I distributed samples of the new brochure to all department heads.**

Certainly it was not "I" who was "retyped and printed in color"!

Right: ***Retyped and printed in color,* the new brochure was distributed to all department heads.**

Retyped and *printed* are past participles.

Checkup 4. Rewrite the sentences to correct any dangling constructions.

1. Writing as quickly as he could, a telephone call interrupted Mr. Perkins.

   ____

2. Talking aloud as she practiced her speech, we could hear Mrs. Moon from across the hall. ______________________________

   ____

3. Bored and tired from his trip, the suitcases began to feel very heavy to Fred.

   ____

4. Dried and withered, I had to throw out the flowers. ______________

   ____

Phrase With Infinitive. Infinitives are verbs such as *to run, to see, to eat, to study, to swim,* and *to buy.* Infinitive phrases generally dangle when the doer of the action is not the subject of the sentence.

Dangling: ***To get the best performance from your air conditioner*, your house should be insulated.**

Will the house get the performance, or will *you*?

Right: ***To get the best performance from your air conditioner,* you should insulate your house.**

Phrase With Verbal Noun. An introductory phrase built around a verbal noun needs a clear subject to modify. Again, make the person who carries out the action the subject of the sentence.

Dangling: ***In investigating energy efficiency*, a shortage of attic insulation was found.**

In the sentence above, the *shortage* appears to be carrying out the investigation.

Right: ***In investigating energy efficiency*, the technician found a shortage of attic insulation.**

Checkup 5. Rewrite the sentences to correct any dangling constructions.

1. To leave work early, your boss's permission will be needed. ______________

2. To understand how a budget is established, Chapter 6 should be read carefully. ______________

3. In asking for more time, my intention was to help the staff. ______________

REVIEW QUIZ

Rewrite the sentences to correct nonparallel or dangling constructions. Write C after sentences that are correct.

1. Having been promoted, my parents gave a party for me. ______________

2. We sat down, uncovered our typewriters, and our reports were begun. ______________

3. Your secretary's notes are more complete than John's. ______________

4. The next speaker is intelligent, controversial, and everyone knows her well. ______________

5. Being made of rubber, I was easily able to bend the hose. ______________

6. In looking over the monthly statement, two errors were quickly found by my accountant. ______________

7. How do these figures compare with last month? ______________

8. We thought we were there to swim, hunt, and for fishing. ______________

9. After closing the door, she came quietly toward the podium. ______

10. After winning my scholarship, my parents gave me a special present.

11. To read most effectively, the light should come from behind your shoulder.

12. Everyone should practice courtesy, cooperation, and consideration. ______

13. In reviewing our goals, several errors were noted. ______

14. While waiting on the corner, a car drove up. ______

15. To improve your story, some suspense should be added. ______

16. Typing, filing, and to write letters take up most of my time. ______

17. We heard the Senator's speech but not the President. ______

18. To research consumers' habits, make decisions, and implementing policies are the main areas of her responsibility. ______

19. To get ahead, good communication skills will be needed by every office worker. ______

20. While filling out the application, my pen fell. ______

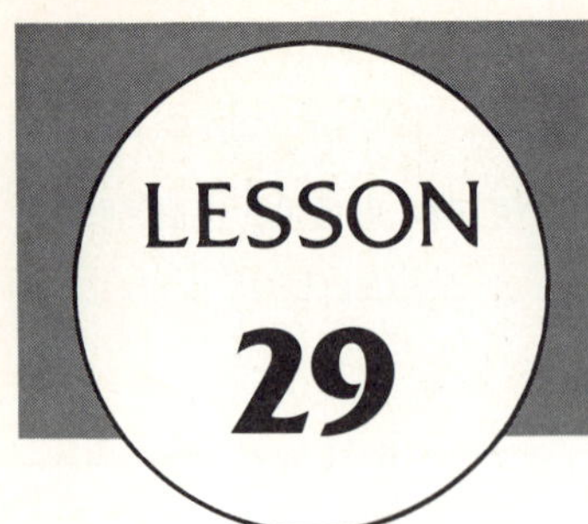

Numbers

When do you use *eight*, *8*, and *8th*? This lesson will give you some general guidelines for using numbers in business correspondence—guidelines that will help you to write messages that are accurate and consistent.

FIGURE STYLE

Generally, in business correspondence numbers from *one* through *ten* are spelled out, and figures (numerals) are used for all other numbers.

Our agency has *six* employees.
She has approved *13* purchase orders.

That rule would be simple if there were no exceptions. But there are some cases that need special treatment.

Related Numbers. Numbers that are related should be treated alike, even if some are above and some below ten.

She supervises *four* secretaries, *two* clerks, *three* typists, and *twelve* account executives.
The purchase order was for *12* bottles of fixative, *16* bottles of dye, and *2* bottles of base.

In the first example, you'd expect *twelve* to be written *12* (because it's over *ten*). But because the other three numbers are below *ten* and thus written out, *twelve* is written out to be consistent. For the same reason, *2* is written in figures in the second example, because the other numbers are over *ten* (and thus written in figures). If most of the related numbers are under *ten*, write them all out; if most are over *ten*, use figures for all.

Remember: This matter of consistency applies only to *related* numbers.

All *three* of us agreed that the *14* store managers should be at the meeting. The number *three* and the number *14* are not related.

Checkup 1. Underline the correct numbers.

1. I typed (six, 6) letters, (three, 3) memos, and (two, 2) reports this morning.
2. So far this year, Ms. Aresti has been absent (four, 4) days, Mr. Billings (eleven, 11) days, and Mrs. May (fourteen, 14) days.
3. We now have (twenty-six, 26) branch offices, but we had only (eight, 8) branches just (four, 4) years ago.

SPECIAL RULES

Numbers Beginning a Sentence. Spell out any number that opens a sentence.

***Eighty-two* people answered, but only *sixty-two* were accepted.** Because the first number is spelled out, the second number—a related number—must also be spelled out.

***Ninety-two* degrees was the temperature.**

Usually, it's a good idea to reword sentences so the numbers don't come first.

Better: **Of the *82* people who answered, only *62* were accepted.** Now both numbers can be expressed in figures, which are preferred.

Better: **The temperature was *92* degrees.**

Neighboring Numbers. When two neighboring numbers are both in figures or both in words, use a comma to separate them. If one of the numbers is part of a compound modifier, spell out the shorter number and use figures for the longer number.

In *1980, 40* branches were in operation. ***Not*:** *In 1980 40 . . . .*
I bought *thirteen 25*-cent pads. ***Not*:** *13 25-cent pads.*

Checkup 2. Underline the correct numbers.

1. (Two hundred, 200) people live in the (nine, 9) buildings.
2. She decorated (four, 4) (thirty-, 30-) room mansions.
3. (Twenty, 20) files were missing.
4. We bought (eleven, 11) (four-, 4-) drawer filing cabinets.

Large Amounts. To make large amounts easy to read, use a combination of figures and words, such as these:

13 million **6 billion** **1.6 million** **2.5 billion**

Indefinite Numbers. Indefinite numbers are always written out.

We sold *hundreds* of boxes. ***Not:*** *100s.*
There were a *few thousand* copies left over. ***Not:*** *few 1,000.*

Checkup 3. Underline the correct numbers.

1. Apparently, (hundreds, 100s) of people were stranded.
2. Last year we shipped (21,000,000, 21 million) cases.
3. A couple of (thousand, 1,000) fans donated ($2,000,000, $2 million).

Addresses. Names of streets from *First* through *Tenth* are written out. Others are expressed in figures. House numbers, except for *One*, are shown in figures.

321 Third Avenue
423 61st Street
2 North Ellen Drive
One 62 Street (*or* One 62d Street)
81 East 21 Avenue

The *st, d,* or *th* may be omitted from the number if a word such as *North* or *West* separates the house number from the street number.

342 West 28 Street (28*th* is unnecessary)

Street or avenue names should not be abbreviated, and commas should not be used in the street, house, or ZIP Code number.

1342 East Seventh Street (***not:*** *1,342 E. Seventh Street)*
Brooklyn, New York 11230 (***not:*** *11,230*)

Checkup 4. Correct any errors in number usage by writing your answers in the space provided.

1. They moved to 1,222 2d Ave. last year. ______________
2. Send the order to 1 So. 10th St., Franklin, IA 26,414. ______________
3. There's a new building at 32 64 Avenue, isn't there? ______________

Money. Definite amounts of money are always given in figures, using the dollar sign for dollars and the word *cent* for cents.

$2.62 **$8** **$4,624** **32 cents**

Notice that no period or zeros follow whole numbers, unless they are listed in columns.

IN A SENTENCE	IN A COLUMN	
I gave the clerk $6 for the scarf.	**$13.25**	
Not: *$6. or $6.00.*	**6.00**	Note zeros for alignment
Coffee is now 25 cents a cup.	**.82**	
Not: *25¢ or $.25.*	**$20.07**	

Checkup 5. Correct any errors in number usage by writing your answers in the space provided.

1. I spent four dollars for a taxi to the airport. ________________
2. Irene thought it would cost $12.00, but the price was $19.98. ________________
3. The $5. fee is very reasonable. ________________

Percentages. Figures are used with the word *percent.* (The symbol % is appropriate only in tabulated lists or statistical work.) No hyphen separates the number and the word *percent.*

Sales are up *6 percent* here and *8.5 percent* in Miami.
A *5 percent* sales tax must be added to this purchase.

Checkup 6. Correct any errors in number usage by writing your answers in the space provided.

1. Only four % of the people voted in the primary. ________________
2. The 13-percent price increase is being argued. ________________
3. About 50% of the work is done by 25% of the staff. ________________

Dates. Dates in business correspondence shouldn't be abbreviated, and they shouldn't be shown as a series of numbers separated by slashes or hyphens.

December 3, 1982 (***Not:*** *Dec. 3, 1982* or *12/3/82*)

When the day follows the month, don't use *st, d,* or *th.*

We bought the building on *June 18* and opened our store on *December 28.* Not: *June 18th* or *December 28th.*

However, when the day comes before the month, *st, d,* or *th* may be used.

We will meet on the *third* of February. ***Or:*** *the 3d of February.*

In month-day-year dates, the year is set off from the rest of the sentence by two commas.

July 4, *1976,* will be long remembered.

Checkup 7. Correct any errors in dates by writing your answers in the space provided.

1. February 26 1973 was the day I joined this government agency. ________________
2. On April 2d and May 13th we held meetings to discuss the agenda. ________________
3. The 14 of Aug. was my birthday; I was born on 8/14/60. ________________

Clock Time. Numbers are used to show clock time, usually with *a.m.* or *p.m.* (note lowercase letters).

He will arrive at *11 a.m.*, and we will meet from *2:30* to *6 p.m.*

Unless you are putting material into tabulated form, don't use zeros when time is "on the hour."

Our work hours are from *8 a.m.* (*not:* 8:00 a.m.) to *4 p.m.* (*not:* 4:00 p.m.).

The word *o'clock* is never used with *a.m.* or *p.m.*

We leave at *6* (or *six*) *o'clock. Not:* at 6 p.m. o'clock.
We leave at *6 p.m. Not:* at 6 p.m. o'clock.

Notice that the hour may be either spelled out or shown in numbers with the word *o'clock.*

Checkup 8. Correct any errors in time by writing your answers in the space provided.

1. She must be at the airport by 4:00 p.m. ________________
2. The bus left at 7:30 a.m., but we were at the depot at 7:00 a.m. o'clock. ________________
3. Come to my office at three o'clock, or call me before 5:00 p.m. ________________

Fractions/Mixed Numbers. Spell out common fractions such as *one-half, one-third,* and so on. Use numerals for fractions such as 11/16, 13/32, and so on. Mixed numbers (a whole number plus a fraction) are usually expressed in numerals.

At least *three-fourths* of our staff members were at the special meeting.
This year's profit was *1¾* times larger than last year's.

Checkup 9. Correct any errors in fractions and mixed numbers by writing your answers in the space provided.

1. I've completed about 2/3 of the report. ________________
2. This machine is three and one-half inches higher than that one. ________________
3. It is only three and two-fifths inches wide. ________________

Let's review the basics.

1. In general, spell out numbers from *one* through *ten*, including street names, and use figures for numbers over *ten.*
2. Treat related numbers the same way.
3. Don't start a sentence with a number.
4. Don't use zeros after even dollar amounts or after numbers showing time "on the hour."

5. Use the symbol for dollars ($), but spell out the word *cents*, except in tables.
6. Use figures with the word *percent*. (*12 percent*, not *12%*)
7. Write out indefinite numbers. (*several hundred people*)
8. Don't add *st, d,* or *th* to the day when it follows the month. (*June 11, August 21*)
9. In month-day-year dates, set off the year with commas. (*March 10, 1982, . . .*)
10. Spell out fractions (*one-third*), but use figures for mixed numbers (2¼).

Are you ready for a quiz?

REVIEW QUIZ

Rewrite the sentences to correct any errors in number usage.

1. His employment date is 11/7/73. ______

   ______

2. Our staff consists of 11 account executives, six secretaries, and two managers. ______

   ______

3. The invoice lists twenty-two boxes of supplies. ______

   ______

4. On April 16 12 visitors will be here for a 2-day conference. ______

   ______

5. I needed 12 25-cent coins for the long-distance calls. ______

   ______

6. Deliver the material to 387 73 Ave. no later than 5 o'clock tomorrow afternoon. ______

   ______

7. 3½ years ago Rose opened her store. ______

   ______

8. We scheduled a conference at 2:00 p.m. o'clock today and one at 6:00 p.m. o'clock tomorrow. ______

   ______

9. The agency increased its profits six and one-half % since last year. ______

   ______

10. The clinic moved from 3d St. to 9th St. ______________________

____

11. We collected a few 100 dollars. ______________________

____

12. Seventeen pages were typed by Roy, and 15 were typed by Adam. ______

____

____

13. We live at 1 East 8th Street, Middle Range, MN 56,321. ______________

____

14. The seventeenth of Jan. is the due date. ______________________

____

15. My share is 1/6, and yours is 2/3. ______________________

____

16. Meet me at 1:00 p.m. on October 1st. ______________________

____

17. We incorporated our business on June 20th, 1976. ______________

____

18. The plane ticket cost $246.00; the hotel room, $42.; and phone calls, 87¢.

____

____

19. She cashed a traveler's check for $100.00 and ran to catch her 11:00 o'clock flight. ______________________

____

20. On 3/1/82 our lease will expire. ______________________

____

SECTION 8 WRAP-UP:
Agreement, Parallelism, and Numbers

REMINDERS

Do your best to avoid these errors!

Error: **The price list for our new products are enclosed.**

The subject of this sentence is *list*, a singular noun. Thus the verb also must be singular.

Correction: **The price list for our new products *is* enclosed.**

Error: **My duties are typing, filing, and to answer the phone.**

Equal sentence parts must be parallel. They must have the same structure. *Typing*, *filing*, and *to answer* are not parallel.

Correction: **My duties are *typing, filing,* and *answering* the phone.**
My duties are *to type, to file,* and *to answer* the phone.

Error: **June 22, 1972 was the date of the letter.**

In month-day-year dates, the year must be set off by *two* commas—one before and one after the year.

Correction: **June 22, 1972, was the date of the letter.**
↑ COMMA HERE!

Error: **The cost for tonight's special dinner (which starts at 7:00 p.m.) is only $15.00 a person.**

No periods, colons, or zeros are used with even dollars or even hours. *Reason*: They are not necessary.

Correction: **The cost for tonight's special dinner (which starts at *7 p.m.*) is only *$15* a person.**

SPELLING EXERCISE

Correct all the misspelled words. Write C below each word that is correctly spelled. Then for each word write a sentence that shows agreement of sentence parts or parallelism or correct number usage. An example is provided. Be prepared for a spelling quiz.

0. jeopordy — Knowing that her job was not in jeopardy,
   jeopardy — she ignored her supervisor's threat.
1. financial
2. vegtable
3. per cent
4. parallel
5. integraty
6. relevent
7. discription
8. araignment
9. amateur
10. embarass
11. foriegn
12. forfit

13. intersede

14. judgemental

15. rythm

INDEX

SURVEY QUIZ
Business English/30

Name ______________________

Date ______________________

PART 1. Are the following groups of words complete sentences? Label each complete sentence *OK.* Then rewrite the other groups of words to make them complete sentences. (Use a separate sheet of paper.) Follow the example.

0. When Mr. Quinlan returns from vacation. When Mr. Quinlan returns from vacation, we will plan an agenda for our seminars.
1. At the beginning of the meeting.
2. Ms. Olsten requested a revised estimate.
3. You have the original copy.
4. Since Mrs. Sanders became district manager.
5. Both shipments will be delayed.
6. On our way to the hotel for dinner.
7. Because she has been a good customer for so many years.
8. The manager's memorandums on the subject of salaries.
9. Six people have ordered this product.
10. I typed it.

Score ______________

PART 2. Underline the correct word in parentheses for each of the following sentences. Then write your answer in the space provided.

1. The reason for the delays (is, are) inexcusable. 1. ______________
2. Cheryl found her wallet (laying, lying) near the elevator. 2. ______________
3. James sometimes acts as if he (was, were) the president of the company. 3. ______________
4. Will the new law (affect, effect) our hiring policy? 4. ______________
5. Did you know about (him, his) canceling tomorrow's meeting? 5. ______________
6. Neither of the customers had (his, their) receipt. 6. ______________
7. Between you and (I, me), I suspect that Janice will become the new district manager. 7. ______________
8. The person (who, whom) you should ask for help is Denise. 8. ______________

9. They recently applied for (a, an) FHA loan. 9. ______

10. This conference room seats (fewer, less) people than I thought it could. 10. ______

11. She is (sure, surely) careful when she uses this machine. 11. ______

12. Suzanne has been (real, really) successful on her new job. 12. ______

13. At the end of the year, the bonus will be divided (among, between) the four department heads. 13. ______

14. The microphone is (in back of, behind) the podium. 14. ______

15. This platform should be (raised, risen) about 3 or 4 inches higher. 15. ______

16. Please send the new catalogs to Ms. Daniels and (I, me). 16. ______

17. Has she (wrote, written) her article on personal finance? 17. ______

18. Do you know whether (there, they're) planning to come to the luncheon tomorrow? 18. ______

19. Several of the people at the meeting (was, were) opposed to the suggestion. 19. ______

20. Because the cloth had (laid, lain) in the sun too long, the color faded. 20. ______

Score ______

PART 3. Correct any errors in the following sentences. Underline each error; then write your correction in the space provided. Write *OK* if a sentence has no error. Follow the examples.

0. Barbara may know where Dr. Oakley went to. 0. went.

00. She never met neither Ann nor Amy. 00. either Ann or

1. Both Andrew and Sonia is invited to the press party. 1. ______

2. Ms. Farber seen the training films at last Monday's production meeting. 2. ______

3. Please help me to take that big box off of the desk. 3. ______

4. Miss O'Rourke, who is one of our account executives, are at a seminar this week. 4. ______

5. Mr. Treat wants we inventory managers to submit weekly reports. 5. ______

SURVEY QUIZ (Continued)

Name ______________________

6. Martin says that the new system works really well. 6. ______
7. One of the women forgot their umbrella in my office. 7. ______
8. Call me whenever there ready to discuss the new production procedures. 8. ______
9. Harold usually don't like to work overtime—especially on weekends. 9. ______
10. Are you sure that Ms. Weems been to Houston before? 10. ______
11. If I were you, I would take a course in finance. 11. ______
12. Mrs. Williams, our supervisor, is the author of several childrens' books. 12. ______
13. The price of this machine is high, but it's efficiency makes the price worthwhile. 13. ______
14. The new model is different from the old one. 14. ______
15. Our manager, as well as her assistants, want to postpone the conference until July or August. 15. ______
16. If you had to choose from among these five applicants, who would you select? 16. ______
17. The invitation states that husbands and wifes of employees are welcome to the dinner. 17. ______
18. Mr. Jeffries approves us postponing the announcement until next May. 18. ______
19. Is there any reasons why we must order this product in such large quantities? 19. ______
20. As your planning the conference, make sure that you order all the audiovisual equipment that you will need. 20. ______

Score ______

PART 4. Add punctuation where needed in the following sentences, and correct any errors in the use of capital letters, numbers, and abbreviations. Follow the examples.

0. "my favorite magazines," said laura, "are business week and time." 0. ______

00. mrs. daly said, "I must leave for chicago as soon as possible; therefore, please reserve a first-class seat on a four thirty flight." 00. 4:30

1. next tuesday march 19th mr holley will visit our canadian office — 1. ________

2. did you know that this years sales have increased fifteen percent over last year's sales — 2. ________

3. in the enclosed brochure see page five you will find a detailed description of this product — 3. ________

4. gloria asked when will the limousine arrive — 4. ________

5. carol francis mark and ralph were assigned to the committee werent they — 5. ________

6. nearly a 1000 people were in the Auditorium to hear our Guest Speaker — 6. ________

7. although dr bradley isnt in the Office now she will return your call later today — 7. ________

8. john loomis who joined our firm last august is a former College Professor — 8. ________

9. I cant believe the tickets cost $35.00 each — 9. ________

10. when she had finished her speech she turned to all of us and said do you have any questions — 10. ________

11. Please correct this ZIP Code number the correct number is 10,020 — 11. ________

12. 6 Field Managers were recently promoted to District Managers — 12. ________

13. you should ask your Doctor for more information on these Vitamins — 13. ________

14. has mister rubin returned from Lunch yet? — 14. ________

15. Roberta received a raise in july nevertheless she will receive another raise soon — 15. ________

16. we have branch offices in ames iowa detroit michigan miami florida and provo utah — 16. ________

17. his sister who is a well known lecturer on international finance lives in utica new york — 17. ________

18. in 1978 432 new franchises were opened — 18. ________

19. karen sarah or vincent should be assigned to this new Project — 19. ________

20. robert j hamilton, jr who is our regional manager is a Graduate of west point — 20. ________

Score ________